GROUND

GROUND RULES

by Eric Chappell

JOSEF WEINBERGER PLAYS

LONDON

GROUND RULES
First published in 2016
by Josef Weinberger Ltd
12-14 Mortimer Street, London W1T 3JJ
www.josef-weinberger.com / plays@jwmail.co.uk

ISBN: 978 0 85676 365 6

Printed by Short Run Press Ltd, Exeter

GROUND RULES was first performed at the Palace Theatre, Westcliffe on 11th October 2014. The cast was as follows:

GERRY HAMMOND	Chris Rees
JUDITH HAMMOND	Sally Lawrence
JO	Sarah Kempton
ASHLEY	Gary McErlane

Directed by Simon Vause
Set and costumes designed by Peter Finlay
Lighting designed by Mat Eldridge-Smith

CAST

in order of appearance:

GERRY HAMMOND	Mid-forties. Round shouldered. Slightly dissipated. Seasoned drinker and clubman.
JUDITH HAMMOND	Mid-forties. Confident, attractive. Primness around the mouth.
JO	Late twenties. Provocatively dressed.
ASHLEY	About thirty-five. Well built. Tanned. Manual worker.

ACT ONE

Scene One

The home of GERRY *and* JUDITH HAMMOND. *Late one summer evening. The room is a large den which overlooks the terrace. There is a fireplace, stage right, with open brickwork. A brick built bar framed with oak beams stands stage left. There are riding trophies on the shelves and rosettes adorn the timbers.*

There is a comfortable sofa, easy chairs and occasional tables. There are bar stools in front of the bar. A telephone stands on the bar. A table with books and papers on it stands upstage by the large window. In front of the window is a long padded window seat. A glass door leads onto the terrace. A door, stage right, leads into the hall.

GERRY HAMMOND *enters from the hall. He is a man in his mid-forties, slightly round shouldered and dissipated in appearance with the air of a seasoned drinker and clubman. He pours a drink then crosses and looks anxiously out of the window.* JUDITH *enters. She is the same age as her husband. She is confident and attractive with a faint primness around her mouth. She is wearing a dark elegant suit and her hair is swept back.*

JUDITH	I'll have one of those.
	(GERRY *pours another drink.*)
GERRY	How is she?
JUDITH	She's had a weep – now she's applying a little make-up.
GERRY	Were there any marks?
JUDITH	Marks? I didn't see any.

GERRY   You said you heard blows.

JUDITH   Well, sort of slaps.

GERRY   I didn't hear slaps.

JUDITH   More like dull thuds. Body blows.

GERRY   (*stares*) Body blows! My God!

JUDITH   He was trying to get her into the car.

GERRY   (*dryly*) Simply opening the door didn't work then?

JUDITH   (*frowns*) I'm glad someone finds it amusing. She was terrified. She was whimpering.

GERRY   Whimpering? (*Frowns.*) I didn't hear whimpering.

JUDITH   You didn't hear much, did you?

GERRY   I was on my way to the car.

JUDITH   She was whimpering. That's why I intervened. I wasn't going to stand by and see a woman subjected to that sort of abuse.

               (GERRY *takes his drink and returns to the window.*)

GERRY   Even so – I don't think it was a good idea to get involved.

JUDITH   Why not?

GERRY   They could be married.

JUDITH   What's that got to do with it? We're married.
                  We don't knock each other about.

GERRY   I know that.

JUDITH   Then tell me what marriage has to do with
                  it?

GERRY   I'll tell you. Remember when I saw that man
                  pushing a woman into the boot of his car in
                  broad daylight? That was assault, abduction
                  and false imprisonment. And I reported it –
                  and what did the police say? "That's alright,
                  sir – they're married". They wouldn't have
                  cared if he'd tied her to the roof rack as long
                  as they were married!

JUDITH   Well, as a matter of fact, they're not
                  married. They're in a relationship.

GERRY   A relationship?

JUDITH   Yes.

GERRY   I knew it! They're living together. That
                  explains it.

JUDITH   Explains what?

GERRY   No stability.

JUDITH   I don't know if they're living together. She's
                  only known him a short time. His name's
                  Ashley.

GERRY   Ashley. Doesn't sound particularly
                  aggressive.

JUDITH   (stares) What did you expect him to be
                  called? Butch? When his parents christened

him Ashley they didn't know he was going
to knock women about.

GERRY   He didn't look particularly aggressive either.

JUDITH   (*dryly*) I didn't realise you got that close to
               him.

GERRY   It was dark but I saw he was taller than me –
               and heavier. Did he have a beard?

JUDITH   No.

GERRY   Must have been the light. I thought he had
               a beard. Still, he seemed to control himself
               pretty well when he saw us. His anger was
               obviously directed against her.

JUDITH   You hoped.

GERRY   In fact, he became restrained – almost
               sheepish.

JUDITH   Sheepish! Gerry, were you listening? He
               called her a tart and a whore and told her to
               find someone else to sleep with.

GERRY   That's my point – he didn't actually swear.
               I think that was out of respect for us. And I
               don't think he'd have said what he did if he
               hadn't been near breaking point.

               (JUDITH *regards him in amazement.*)

JUDITH   You know, if you go on like this I think I'll
               grow to like him. He was assaulting her,
               Gerry.

GERRY   Then why didn't we take her to the police
               station as I suggested?

(*He pours another drink.*)

JUDITH   Because she wanted to go to her sister's.

GERRY   Her sister wasn't in.

JUDITH   She's going to ring her in a few minutes.

GERRY   And suppose her sister doesn't come home tonight? Suppose she's out having a stormy relationship somewhere? These things tend to run in families. Her sister could be doing three rounds with someone right now.

JUDITH   Then she'll have to stay here. She can't go home. He has a key.

GERRY   They are living together! And we're interfering – keeping them apart. Poor old Ashley could be there right now with his head stuck in the gas oven.

JUDITH   He's not.

GERRY   How do you know?

JUDITH   Because he followed us.

          (GERRY *almost chokes on his drink.*)

GERRY   What!

          (*He starts to take out a cigarette.*)

JUDITH   Not in the house, darling.

          (*He returns the cigarette to the packet.*)

GERRY   (*anxiously*) Followed us?

JUDITH   When we stopped at her sister's – he was behind us. Didn't you see his lights?

GERRY   No – I was looking for the house. I knew it! I knew we should have gone to the police station.

JUDITH   She didn't want that.

GERRY   But he could have followed us back here.

JUDITH   No, I think he pulled off.

GERRY   You think he pulled off! And suppose he didn't? Suppose he comes back here and smashes the place up?

JUDITH   (*mockingly*) Not Ashley. He respects us.

GERRY   Yes, and I don't want to lose that respect. Don't forget he's younger and bigger than I am. Much younger and much bigger, Judith.

JUDITH   Gerry, you've been ageing and shrinking ever since this happened. I just wonder what you'd have done if I hadn't been there.

GERRY   (*hesitates*) I'd have reported it.

JUDITH   (*disgusted*) Reported it.

GERRY   You know I'm not confrontational. If you'd wanted someone confrontational you should have married Ashley.

JUDITH   A man who attacks women? Stop worrying. We've done the right thing. And when she's calmed down I'm going to have a serious talk with her.

GERRY   (*groans*) Not one of your serious talks.

JUDITH   What do you mean?

GERRY   Nothing – but do you think she'll listen? They say there are some women who enjoy this sort of thing.

JUDITH   Who says? That's the sort of thing men say.

GERRY   I've heard women say it.

JUDITH   Well, I don't want to hear you say it. Are you suggesting that poor old Ashley hits her because she enjoys it and that he'd much sooner spend a quiet evening by the fire?

GERRY   Well, you must admit there's something about her . . .

JUDITH   What?

GERRY   I thought that skirt was rather short – there were a couple of buttons undone – and she paints her toenails.

JUDITH   Well, you may not have seen Ashley clearly but you certainly got a good look at Jo.

GERRY   Jo?

JUDITH   That's her name. So, you thought she was asking for it?

GERRY   I meant that women who dress provocatively do invite that sort of thing.

JUDITH   Well, that doesn't say much for the human race, does it? It certainly doesn't say much for men. Did you feel the urge to strike her?

GERRY   No.

JUDITH   Not even when you saw the painted toenails?

GERRY   No!

JUDITH   I'd point out that there were two parties to
            that quarrel and she was the one who came
            out of it with dignity – even if she does
            paint her toenails.

GERRY   What does she do for a living?

JUDITH   I don't know. I didn't ask. (*Frowns.*) I
            thought there was something familiar about
            her.

GERRY   (*darkly*) Is she a hairdresser?

JUDITH   I don't know. Why? Do hairdressers get
            beaten up regularly. Are we establishing a
            pattern here?

GERRY   Not really – it was just that you said there
            was something familiar about her. (*Pause.*)
            What does he do?

JUDITH   Why do you want to know what everyone
            does?

GERRY   Probably a manual worker. Good build –
            clean limbed.

JUDITH   Clean limbed! You thought he had a beard!

GERRY   I mean he looked decent enough. She
            probably brought the worst out of him.

JUDITH   If she did it must have been there in the first
            place. We have to find out why.

GERRY (*sighs*) You're going to counsel them, aren't you?

JUDITH Why not? That's what I do.

GERRY Don't you think you do enough? Broken marriages – the criminally damaged – the mentally unstable – the suicidal – the bereaved. If you don't get them at one end you get them at the other. Sometimes twice!

JUDITH It's what I do best. I feel I make a difference. I think I can help these two. They looked perfectly happy when they were sitting together in the bar.

GERRY Were they eating?

JUDITH I don't know. Why?

GERRY If he was buying her a meal – it shows he thought something of her. She wasn't a casual pick-up.

JUDITH (*sighs*) We're back to those toenails again. I've told you – they're in a relationship.

GERRY So she says. All we know is that you heard slaps and whimpers. And there are no marks.

JUDITH He called her a tart, Gerry.

GERRY Perhaps she is. Anyway, he was in a passion. And where passion's concerned – we have to make allowances. The French do.

JUDITH The French also drink a lot of red wine. Besides which, you can always depend on the French to behave badly. Because Jo's

been involved in a brawl doesn't mean she
invited it. Don't you realise that victims of
violence often feel guilty because they think
they've provoked it. That's why it doesn't
always get reported.

(*She becomes aware of* GERRY *drumming his
fingers*.)

Don't drum your fingers, darling, You know
how it irritates. You're attitude's typical –
you should have been a judge. We shouldn't
condemn her – we should be helping her to
recover her self-esteem.

(*Her voice trails away as* JO *enters the room
hesitantly from the hall.* JO *is attractive and
in her late twenties. Despite what* GERRY
*has said, her clothes are in good taste, if a
little revealing.* GERRY *gives her toenails an
involuntary glance.*)

JO   (*uncertainly*) I thought I heard voices . . .

JUDITH   Come in, Jo. Let me take your coat. This is
            the den. You'll be forgiven for thinking it's a
            pub. That was Gerry's idea. Can he get you
            a drink?

JO   No, I think I've had enough.

GERRY   Ah, one too many, hey?

JUDITH   (*frowns*) Jo said she'd had enough – not one
            too many, darling. How do you feel now, Jo?

JO   Embarrassed.

JUDITH   Don't be. (*She gives* JO's *arm a squeeze.*)
            We understand. We've only known you a

short time, Jo, but we know you're a lovely person.

(GERRY *stares at* JUDITH *incredulously*.)

These things happen.

JO But why do they always happen to me?

GERRY (*quickly*) Do they?

JUDITH (*giving* GERRY *a sharp glance*) Had he been drinking heavily?

JO Not in the pub – he may have had some before he came in.

GERRY So you met in the bar?

JUDITH (*acidly*) Jo didn't say that, darling, but does it matter?

GERRY I just wondered how it started. Whether Jo was in there, sitting at the bar, having a quiet drink – nothing wrong with that – and he came in and tried to pick her up.

JUDITH I thought I'd made it clear, darling, that Jo and Ashley are acquainted.

JO We did come in together – in a way . . .

JUDITH In a way?

JO I realised he was following me – so I slipped into the pub to avoid him. But he saw my car and came in and accused me of meeting someone.

GERRY	Were you?
JUDITH	(*frowns*) So your car's still in the car park?
JO	Yes, it's safer there.
GERRY	Because you've been drinking?

(JUDITH *sighs again*.)

JO	No – but the last time this happened he drove me off the road.

(*They both stare at her in surprise.*)

JUDITH	Drove you off the road. How?
JO	He rammed me.
JUDITH	Rammed you!
GERRY	Does he suffer from road rage?
JO	He suffers from road rage, car park rage, public house rage and restaurant rage. You name it. It doesn't take much. He could start a fight in an empty room.

(GERRY *crosses and looks nervously out of the window.*)

JUDITH	Jo, how did you get involved with someone so unpredictable?
JO	It's a long story.
JUDITH	(*smiles*) We have plenty of time – perhaps you'd like to talk to me about it whilst my husband makes some coffee . . .

*(She crosses to the table and deftly slides
pencil and pad into her hand.)*

GERRY   Judith's a counsellor.

JO   *(uneasily)* Oh.

JUDITH   Don't look at me like that, Jo. I hate the
              word too. I'm a listener, that's all. It's for
              you to find your own solutions. I'm merely a
              conduit between one person and another.

              (She sits JO *in an easy chair and pulls
              up a stool. She crouches attentively. And
              becomes aware of* GERRY *standing behind
              her and regarding the scene with interest.
              she gives him a sharp glance.* GERRY *drifts
              towards the door.)*

              Tell me, what caused this outburst tonight?

              *(*GERRY *drifts back.)*

              I thought I saw you sitting at the bar,
              laughing and joking.

JO   We were.

JUDITH   And he had an affectionate arm on your
              shoulder.

JO   He had. We'd made it up. He agreed his
              suspicions were groundless.

JUDITH   Then what happened? How did this display
              of affection degenerate into the scene I
              witnessed in the car park?

JO   *(pause)* You know there's a free salad trolley
              in the restaurant?

(JUDITH *stares uncomprehendingly.*)

JUDITH   A free salad trolley?

JO   In the restaurant. Well, we were having
                jumbo scampi and French fries in the bar . . .

JUDITH   Yes?

JO   And I said I'd like some salad from the
                salad trolley in the restaurant. And he said I
                couldn't because we were eating in the bar.
                But I said if we'd ordered a dish from the
                restaurant menu we were entitled to a free
                salad from the salad trolley even though we
                were eating in the bar.

                (JUDITH *continues to stare.*)

GERRY   I think you're right.

                (JUDITH *gives him an irritated glance.*)

JO   And since the scampi was on the restaurant
                menu and not the bar menu I went to get
                some salad.

GERRY   I'd have done the same.

                (JUDITH *sighs.*)

JO   He watched me in silence. When I got to
                the salad trolley I met this charming man.
                I don't know if you saw him? Tall, guards
                officer type, dark curly hair in the nape of
                his neck?

JUDITH   No.

JO   Anyway, he agreed with me that if you
              ordered from the restaurant menu – even one
              dish – you were entitled to a free salad from
              the salad trolley. In fact, we were laughing
              about it when I looked back and saw these
              angry, bloodshot eyes staring at me.

GERRY   Ashley?

JO   Yes. And when I got back to the bar he
              accused me of belittling him as a man – of
              going to the salad trolley just to meet the
              guards officer type – of coming into the pub
              to meet him – and finally of having a long
              standing affair with him.

JUDITH   (*incredulously*) All this because of a salad?

JO   Yes.

JUDITH   I find that incredible.

GERRY   Salad trolley rage.

JUDITH   (*acid sweet*) Darling, weren't you going to
              make the coffee?

GERRY   You always say my coffee's awful.

              (JUDITH *sighs and puts down her pad.*)

JUDITH   Very well. I'll get the coffee – then we'll
              talk. No problem's insoluble – not even this
              one.

JO   Are you sure?

JUDITH   I want you to look upon this as a new
              beginning, JO – the first day of the rest of
              your life.

(*She pats* Jo's *shoulder and exits.*)

GERRY   You've got her going now. She loves this
         sort of thing.

JO   I wish I did. (*Pause.*) What's your name
         again?

GERRY   Gerry.

JO   I'd forgotten. I suppose because she calls
         you darling all the time.

GERRY   She doesn't.

JO   She did in front of me.

GERRY   Yes – probably wanted to give an impression
         of togetherness.

JO   But it doesn't.

GERRY   Doesn't it?

JO   Anyone can be darling. There's only one you
         – that's Gerry.

GERRY   That's true.

         (*He studies her closely.*)

JO   What are you staring at?

GERRY   Judith said she heard blows.

JO   That's right.

GERRY   Several blows.

JO   Yes.

GERRY   But there aren't any marks.

JO   How do you know there aren't any marks?
                He's not a fool – he wouldn't mark me where
                it would show. (*Darkly.*) There'll be bruises.

GERRY   Will there?

JO   Of course there will. Do you want to see?

GERRY   No – not really . . . (*Pauses.*) . . . On the
                other hand . . . Perhaps they should be
                witnessed . . .

                (JO *pulls out her shirt and raises it slowly.
                They scrutinise her skin closely.*)

JO   There should be some somewhere . . .

                (*She lifts her shirt a little higher.*)

GERRY   (*huskily*) Yes, I think I see a bruise.

JO   And there'll be finger marks on my
                shoulder. He's got fingers like pincers.

                (*She drops her shirt undoes a button and
                exposes her shoulder.*)

GERRY   Oh, yes . . .

                (*He looks deep inside her shirt.*)

                Is that a butterfly?

JO   Yes.

(*Whilst this is happening the broad figure of* ASHLEY *appears at the window.*)

GERRY   Is it a tattoo?

JO   No, it's a transfer – it comes off. I wouldn't mark my body permanently – I leave that to Ashley. Do you like it?

GERRY   Yes – it sort of moves, doesn't it?

JO   I've several more.

GERRY   Have you?

JO   Would you like to . . . (*Hesitates.*) No, perhaps not. (*She tucks her shirt in.*) Ashley's mad about them.

GERRY   You put them on for him?

JO   No – he puts them on.

GERRY   Does he?

JO   While I'm sleeping. Butterflies. Bluebirds. Serpents. In the most unexpected places – you wouldn't imagine. I can wake up covered in graffiti.

GERRY   Yes . . .

(GERRY *continues to stare into her shirt watched by* ASHLEY *from the shadows.* JO *meets* GERRY'S *eyes for a moment. Silence. She buttons her shirt.*)

JO   I think I'd better phone my sister again.

GERRY   Use the one in the study.

                         *(They enter into the hall. There is a
                         splintering sound as the door to the terrace
                         is forced open.* ASHLEY *enters breathing
                         heavily and obviously under strong emotion.
                         He is well built, about thirty-five. He is
                         tanned and well-groomed but still retains
                         the outdoor appearance of a manual worker.
                         He stares moodily about him. He picks up
                         the phone and rips it savagely from the wall
                         then replaces it on the bar. He slumps into a
                         chair.*

                         GERRY *returns and crosses to the bar
                         without noticing* ASHLEY. *He chuckles at
                         the memory of what has just happened.
                         He is watched by* ASHLEY. *He is about to
                         pour himself another drink when he feels a
                         draught from the door. Frowns and crosses
                         and examines the door in bewilderment.*

                         ASHLEY *stands.* GERRY *turns. He sees* ASHLEY
                         and almost has a heart attack. He swallows.)

GERRY   It's you. It's Ashley, isn't it?

ASHLEY   Yes.

GERRY   You can't come in here.

ASHLEY   I'm in.

GERRY   But you shouldn't be. It's against the law.

ASHLEY   What is?

GERRY   Coming into someone's house like this.

ASHLEY   No, it isn't.

GERRY   Isn't it?

ASHLEY   Not unless you cause damage.

GERRY   You've caused damage. You've damaged the
                 door.

ASHLEY   Do you think I care?

GERRY   That's not the point. I must ask you to leave.

ASHLEY   Ask away.

                 (ASHLEY *sits*.)

GERRY   Ashley, you can't stay here. Not after what
                 she said.

                 (ASHLEY *rises abruptly.* GERRY *becomes
                 aware of his superior height and falls back*.)

ASHLEY   I knew it! You're already on her side. You've
                 taken her word for everything. That's what
                 she does.

GERRY   (*soothingly*) Ashley, I'm not on her side.
                 And if it was left to me you could stay as
                 long as you like. We could talk about this.
                 But it's the wife . . . (*He looks hopefully
                 towards the door.*) She'd be furious if she
                 knew you'd just barged in – then there's
                 the damage to the door, she won't like that.
                 (*Hastily.*) Not that I'm going to tell her.
                 Because I sympathise. I understand. I know
                 what you're going through. I've been there
                 myself.

                 (ASHLEY *looks at him in surprise*.)

ASHLEY   You have?

GERRY   I know what it's like. We're both emotional
               men – easily hurt. Have a drink. Scotch?

               (ASHLEY *nods but doesn't take his eyes off*
               GERRY.)

               And don't think for a moment that she's
               pulled the wool over my eyes. Soda?

               (ASHLEY *shakes his head.*)

               No – the jury's still out as far as I'm
               concerned.

               (*He hands* ASHLEY *his drink.*)

               And I certainly didn't believe every word
               she said.

               (ASHLEY *puts his drink down.*)

ASHLEY   What did she say?

GERRY   (*nervously*) What?

ASHLEY   What did she say about me?

GERRY   (*hesitates*) She said you hit her.

ASHLEY   Hit her! Wouldn't you have hit her?

GERRY   (*cautiously*) I don't know. Who's to say? I
               might. It depends.

ASHLEY   If she ruined your life?

GERRY   If she ruined my life I'd certainly hit her.
               But has she ruined your life? Surely that's
               open for discussion.

ASHLEY   Listen. I walked out on my family. I took
                out a second mortgage on an expensive
                apartment. I fully furnished it. And all for
                her because that's what she wanted. Then
                I get laid off and she goes to her sister's.
                I'm ruined. My only hope's the lottery – my
                future's probably the river.

GERRY   (*appalled*) You were laid off and she walked
                out? I think you're better off without her.

ASHLEY   I can't live without her.

                (GERRY *pats* ASHLEY'S *shoulder.*)

GERRY   I thought that once, Ashley – over twenty
                years ago – I felt just like you do now –
                never thought I'd get over it. But I did. Oh,
                there's an aching emptiness sometimes –
                the occasional pang. (*Pause.*) This is just
                between you and me of course.

ASHLEY   Of course.

GERRY   I know what it's like to be treated like
                you've been treated, Ashley.

ASHLEY   What did she do?

                (GERRY *shakes his head.*)

                That bad?

GERRY   Put the phone down on me.

                (ASHLEY *stares incredulously.*)

ASHLEY   Is that all?

GERRY   I was talking. It was like a thunderclap. I
             can still hear it.

ASHLEY   Then what happened?

GERRY   Nothing.

ASHLEY   Nothing?

GERRY   Never saw her again. I knew when I wasn't
             wanted. And that's my point. We don't
             always get what we want in this life, Ashley.

ASHLEY   I do.

GERRY   (*surprised*) Do you?

ASHLEY   I wouldn't have left it like that. (*Pause.*)
             Why was she stripping off?

GERRY   (*alarmed*) What?

             (*He takes out a cigarette. His hand is
             trembling nervously. He remembers and
             slips the cigarette back.*)

ASHLEY   Why was she stripping off? Just now.

GERRY   She wasn't stripping off. She was showing
             me her bruises. And I have to say I was
             shocked, Ashley. In my darkest moments –
             and I've had a few – I have never struck a
             woman.

ASHLEY   Never?

GERRY   No.

ASHLEY   Has a woman struck you?

GERRY　　　Well, no.

ASHLEY　　Did you see me strike her?

GERRY　　　We heard blows.

ASHLEY　　Did you see the blows?

GERRY　　　No.

ASHLEY　　They weren't all mine. I was on the
　　　　　　defensive. Let me show you something. (*He
　　　　　　rolls up his sleeve.*) See that?

GERRY　　　(*looks*) Yes – looks nasty.

ASHLEY　　Steam iron.

GERRY　　　Why?

ASHLEY　　Jealousy. She stores things up. She's
　　　　　　vindictive. And then it's the steam iron.

GERRY　　　Then you're better off without her.

ASHLEY　　Why do you keep saying that?

GERRY　　　What?

ASHLEY　　That I'd be better off without her.

GERRY　　　Well, that's how it strikes me, as a casual
　　　　　　observer . . .

ASHLEY　　(*broodingly*) When you say I'd be better off
　　　　　　without her you don't know how terrific she
　　　　　　can be . . .

GERRY　　　Terrific?

ASHLEY   I've never known anyone like her.

GERRY   You haven't?

ASHLEY   And I've been around.

GERRY   (*pause*) That terrific?

ASHLEY   Unbelievable. And I've known some women.

GERRY   (*pause*) But she's the most . . . terrific?

ASHLEY   No comparison, er . . .

             (*He gestures towards* GERRY.)

GERRY   Gerry.

ASHLEY   Gerry.

             (GERRY *and* ASHLEY *drink in silence.*)

GERRY   That terrific?

ASHLEY   And when she wants you to love her . . .

GERRY   You can't resist?

ASHLEY   No chance. She starts with her eyes.

GERRY   Her eyes?

ASHLEY   She looks at you and draws you in. They're
             like deep pools. Know what I mean?

GERRY   I know what you mean.

ASHLEY   And they get deeper and deeper until you're
             drowning but you don't care – you don't

want to be saved. And then you're floating
. . . and she's moving over you in waves . . .

(*He becomes lost in thought.*)

GERRY   (*encouragingly*) That terrific?

ASHLEY   Lobster thermidor, Gerry.

GERRY   (*stares*) Lobster thermidor?

ASHLEY   Something you don't get at home. Know
what I mean?

GERRY   I know what you mean, Ashley.

ASHLEY   The trouble is, I have this feeling that one
day I'm going to look back on this and be
dead miserable. Because you can't hold onto
it, Gerry. It's, what's the word?

GERRY   (*huskily*) Fleeting.

ASHLEY   That's it – fleeting. And you can't get it out
on video. Well, you can . . . but it's not the
same.

GERRY   But does it have to be fleeting?

ASHLEY   Oh, yes – because you see, she's a gypsy.

(GERRY *almost laughs, then checks himself.*)

GERRY   A gypsy?

ASHLEY   On her mother's side. Her mother was pure
gypsy. Her great grandfather came here in a
painted caravan. And once a gypsy . . .

(ASHLEY *shrugs*.)

GERRY   What do you mean – once a gypsy?

ASHLEY   The call of the open road, Gerry – leaving
               behind a broken heart. You see, once you've
               kissed a gypsy woman – you're finished.

GERRY   Are you?

ASHLEY   You never get over it. It's well known.

GERRY   But she's only half gypsy.

ASHLEY   Not in the moonlight. (*He sighs and looks in
               the direction of the hall.*) Where is she? I've
               got to see her. I can't help myself.

GERRY   (*nervously*) The wife doesn't think that's a
               good idea, Ashley.

ASHLEY   Why do you say that? The wife. I mean she's
               your wife, no one else's.

GERRY   Well, yes.

ASHLEY   So why don't you say my wife?

GERRY   I don't know.

ASHLEY   She's the woman who intervened, isn't she?
               The one in the dark suit and the unflinching
               stare?

GERRY   That's her.

ASHLEY   Dead elegant. (*Looks at rosettes*.) Does she
               ride?

GERRY   Yes, and shoots and fences. She's a great believer in violent exercise.

ASHLEY   Nice eyes. Grey, aren't they?

GERRY   (*hesitates*) Grey? I'm not quite sure.

ASHLEY   (*stares*) You don't know the colour of her eyes?

GERRY   Not to be definite.

ASHLEY   They're grey, all right. (*Pause.*) What's her star sign?

GERRY   I'm not sure.

ASHLEY   (*stares*) You don't know her star sign.

GERRY   I did know once.

ASHLEY   I'm a great believer in star signs. They have to be compatible. If they're not compatible – you're wasting your time.

GERRY   Are you?

ASHLEY   You could have been wasting your time all these years.

GERRY   I didn't know that. (*He looks towards the hall again.*) Is she across there?

GERRY   Who?

ASHLEY   Jo. Where is she?

GERRY   I don't think I can tell you that.

ASHLEY   I'm calmer now.

GERRY   No – I'm sorry.

ASHLEY   If you don't tell me – I'll smash the place
                up.

GERRY   She's in the study – across the hall.

                (ASHLEY *crosses to the door and turns.*)

ASHLEY   Yes – definitely grey.

                (*He exits.* GERRY *looks cautiously after*
                ASHLEY. *He picks up the handset from the
                bar and backs towards window. Starts to
                make a call then realises he's trailing a
                loose cable behind him. Groans. He returns
                the phone to the bar as* JUDITH *enters with
                the coffee.*)

JUDITH   Where is she?

GERRY   Ringing her sister.

JUDITH   (*turns*) I'll fetch her.

GERRY   I wouldn't.

JUDITH   Why not?

GERRY   He's here.

JUDITH   What!

GERRY   So I'd take those coffee cups back and bring
                mugs. He may smash the place up.

JUDITH   And you let him through there?

GERRY   I didn't have much choice. Besides, he's calmer now.

JUDITH   How did he get in?

GERRY   He forced the door.

(*She crosses to examine the door then returns and picks up the phone.*)

GERRY   What are you going to do?

JUDITH   Ring the police.

GERRY   You'll have to reconnect it. He's pulled it out of the socket.

(JUDITH *examines the loose cable.*)

JUDITH   And you say he's calmer. He doesn't seem very calm to me.

GERRY   He's calmed down since then. He only wants to talk.

JUDITH   Talk! He could be strangling her!

(*She takes out mobile phone. There's a scream.* Jo *backs into the room. She is holding a telephone with the cable trailing.* ASHLEY *follows her.*)

Jo   Look what he's done – ripped the phone out.

ASHLEY   All I wanted was five minutes. Five minutes out of a lifetime. Is that too much to ask?

Jo   It is with you. Five minutes is a lifetime.

ASHLEY   That's a cheap remark.

JO   What do you expect from a tart.

ASHLEY   I didn't mean that.

                (*He moves forward. She flinches from him.*)

                And stop flinching!

JO   I'll flinch if I want to. If you're frightened
                of what they'll think – it's too late. They
                saw you hitting me. They know what you're
                like.

GERRY   (*desperately*) Try and stay calm, Ashley.

ASHLEY   I am calm. Just stay out of this, Gerry.

                (JO *moves behind* GERRY.)

JO   Watch out for those big fists.

ASHLEY   I haven't got big fists. I've got sensitive
                hands.

JO   Sensitive. You've got fingers like bananas.

                (ASHLEY *moves forward as* JO *retreats
                further behind* GERRY. GERRY *tries to save
                his drink.*)

JUDITH   (*in a loud voice*) Stop!

                (*They all turn towards* JUDITH *in surprise.*)

                No one is going to attack anyone in this
                house. For good or ill you're our guests. I
                would ask you to respect that.

(They look subdued.)

Now, I think it would be a good idea if
Gerry stood between you until you're in
control of your feelings.

(GERRY *looks worried.*)

GERRY   Are you sure, Judith?

JUDITH   Please, darling.

(GERRY *stands reluctantly between* ASHLEY
and JO.)

JUDITH   I think the problem here is mainly one of
communication.

GERRY   I thought they were communicating pretty
well, Judith.

JUDITH   That wasn't communication – that was
conflict. You two are not really saying what
you feel.

JO   I'm saying what I feel, all right.

JUDITH   You're so busy looking for things you
dislike about each other, you've forgotten
the things that attracted you in the first place.

GERRY   Er, I think Ashley knows what attracted
him, Judith . . .

JUDITH   Do you mind, darling? I'm referring to the
good things. The things we call pleasers.
These are the positive things in your
relationship. The trouble is your thoughts
are negative – you're compiling a list of
failings.

Jo	I don't need to compile a list. I can say it in one word. Vanity.
ASHLEY	Vanity! (*Fiercely.*) If I was vain do you think I'd be chasing after you?
	(GERRY *looks anxious and protects his drink again.*)
JUDITH	You see – it's not that you can't articulate – it's that you can't communicate. You can't really express what concerns you. That's why you need a sympathetic ear.
GERRY	(*quietly*) She means hers.
JUDITH	Now, darling, would you take Ashley into the study whilst Jo and I have a little chat. (*Smiles.*) Don't worry, Ashley – we won't drive off into the night.
ASHLEY	You can't. My car's blocking the end of the drive.
Jo	You should have been in the SAS.
JUDITH	(*firmly*) If you don't mind, Ashley.
	(ASHLEY *moves reluctantly towards the door.* GERRY *follows with the drinks.*)
GERRY	(*reproachfully*) Perhaps you'd bring the telephone, Ashley.
	(ASHLEY *picks up the phone.*)
ASHLEY	What are you going to talk about?
Jo	Your favourite subject – you.

JUDITH   (*quickly*) I want to find out what's in Jo's
              mind.

ASHLEY   Well that shouldn't take long.

              (*As he exits,* JO *picks up a cushion to throw.*
              JUDITH *catches her arm.*)

JUDITH   Come and sit down, Jo.

              (*She guides* JO *back to the chair.*)

              You may think this is a waste of time but I
              can assure you it isn't. I'm experienced in
              these matters.

JO   You'll need to be to sort this mess out.

JUDITH   Oh, I won't sort this mess out – that's up
              to you. I'll merely help you to identify
              the mess. (*She deftly retrieves the pad
              and pencil from the table.*) I'm not in the
              business of keeping people together who'd
              sooner be apart. It's for you to evaluate
              your relationship and decide if it's worth
              preserving for the good things in it. After
              all, no relationship is perfect.

JO   What about yours?

JUDITH   (*smiles*) We're talking about your
              relationship, Jo. You mentioned a word a
              moment ago that I found illuminating. The
              word was vanity.

JO   Yes.

JUDITH   You think he's vain?

JO   Don't you? Didn't you see the way he was
              trying to catch a glimpse of himself in
              the double glazing. And that lock of hair's
              not natural – he teases it out. He spends a
              fortune on clothes. He'd sooner dress than
              eat. He's always in debt. And he's a control
              freak. He has to be right about everything.
              Ask him about the free salad with the
              scampi.

JUDITH   (*soothingly*) I intend to ask him about the
              free salad with the scampi – in fact, I think
              it's highly significant. (*Pause.*) Jo, I've
              heard you list his shortcomings with great
              penetration. Don't you feel this may make
              him feel inadequate?

JO   He doesn't feel inadequate – he is
              inadequate. The trouble is he doesn't know
              it. He thinks everyone loves him. He thinks
              he's God's gift to women. It's going to be
              the biggest disappointment of his life when
              he finds out he's not.

JUDITH   He thinks women admire him?

JO   He thinks they can't resist him. You should
              see him on the scaffolding.

JUDITH   Scaffolding?

JO   He's a scaffolder – that's when he's working
              – which isn't very often. The sun's only got
              to peep through the clouds and he's off with
              his shirt – out comes the comb – then the
              teasing. Then he's flexing his muscles and
              swinging from the bars like a monkey – and
              shouting after the office girls. He thinks
              he's spreading a little happiness – all he's
              spreading is embarrassment.

(*She pauses for breath again.* JUDITH *is silent for a moment.*)

JUDITH   (*quietly*) You're frightened of losing him, aren't you?

JO   (*stares*) What?

JUDITH   That's why you're finding fault. You want to damage his self-esteem. Undermine his confidence. You think in that way you can keep him.

JO   You must be joking.

JUDITH   Jo, you've talked about him at length. You haven't mentioned one good point. Why? There must have been something that drew you to him in the first place. What are his good points?

                  (*There is an unpromising silence.*)

                  There must be some. What attracted you?

JO   That's obvious, isn't it? His physique. I've always been attracted to the physical. That's been my downfall. I've always gone by looks. You must have noticed his looks.

JUDITH   Not really.

JO   He will be disappointed.

JUDITH   Well, I haven't seen him to his best advantage this evening.

JO   No – you haven't seen his smile. When he smiles at you he can make your heart leap. You feel you're the only woman in the room.

He's got a smile that would make a nun snap her rosary.

(JUDITH *sips her drink for a moment.*)

JUDITH   That's quite a smile . . .

JO   I can watch him for hours. In the bedroom getting dressed . . . getting undressed . . .

              (*There's another silence.* JUDITH *realises she's broken her point. She reaches for the pencil sharpener.*)

              He has this thing about his legs but . . .

JUDITH   His legs?

JO   He had rickets or something when he was young. He's always studying them in the mirror. But they look great to me.

              (JUDITH *becomes busy with the sharpener.*)

JUDITH   Well, we're certainly finding some good points now, Jo.

JO   And he doesn't just look good – he is good. He can make you feel . . .

JUDITH   What?

JO   He plays with a full deck, Judith – if you know what I mean . . .

JUDITH   I know what you mean.

(JUDITH *discovers with surprise how low she is on the pencil. Selects another one. She commences sharpening again.*)

JUDITH   Well, I don't think you have much to complain about there, Jo. And does he ever lose his temper in these situations?

JO   No, he's kind and caring.

JUDITH   That's because he can express himself in his love-making. He's confident, skilled, assured . . .

            (*She continues sharpening. It has become frantic.*)

JO   Tell me about it! He's assured, all right. He's also vain, conceited, bad-tempered and a control freak!

JUDITH   Is that why you walked out?

JO   (*pause*) No – it was because I found a lipstick in the bedroom and it wasn't mine.

JUDITH   Did you ask him about the lipstick?

JO   Yes. He said he didn't know anything about it.

JUDITH   But you don't believe him?

JO   No.

JUDITH   And this is corroding your relationship.

JO   Well, it's not helping.

JUDITH   If there was someone . . .

Jo   I know there was someone.

JUDITH   If he was honest about it, and told you.
                Would you forgive him?

Jo   Forgive him!

                (*She rises to her feet.*)

JUDITH   Would you take him back?

Jo   (*pause*) Yes. Now I know someone else
                wants him – I want him more than ever.

JUDITH   That's not unusual. You see someone else
                has put a value on him.

                (*She pats* Jo's *shoulder.*)

                I think all your relationship needs is a little
                honesty. Would you ask Ashley to pop
                through for a moment?

                (Jo *begins to cross and pauses.*)

Jo   You know a lot about this don't you?

JUDITH   It's what I do.

Jo   Judith, all these ideas you have – they're
                very clever but do they work?

JUDITH   Jo, Gerry and I have been married over
                twenty years – you don't see us throwing the
                furniture at each other, do you?

Jo   (*smiles*) No.

(JO *exits.* JUDITH *looks surprised at how
short her pencil has become. she reaches for
another as* ASHLEY *enters the room.*)

ASHLEY   (*sulkily*) What do you want?

JUDITH   Close the door, Ashley. And come and sit
              down.

              (ASHLEY *does so reluctantly.*)

              Good news. She loves you.

ASHLEY   Did she say that?

JUDITH   Not exactly.

ASHLEY   She wouldn't. She's frightened of the word.

JUDITH   Well, she's not frightened of much else . . .
              She was very frank.

              (ASHLEY *smiles for the first time.*)

ASHLEY   What did she say?

              (JUDITH *regards his smile curiously for a
              moment and commences sharpening.*)

JUDITH   That you have a good physical relationship.

ASHLEY   She said that?

JUDITH   Yes. Do you mind if I make notes?

ASHLEY   Not at all. (*Pause.*) She's right, of course.
              That's because I'm a giver.

JUDITH   A giver. This is interesting. You see yourself
            as a giver?

ASHLEY   I've always been a giver .

JUDITH   What exactly do you mean by giving?

ASHLEY   A giver makes someone happy. That's all a
            giver wants to do. (*Broodingly.*) But most
            people are takers. There are only two types
            of people really – givers and takers.

JUDITH   And is Jo a giver?

            (ASHLEY *considers for a moment.*)

ASHLEY   No, she's a taker. Oh, she pretends to be
            a giver – and sometimes you think she's
            giving – but actually she's taking.

JUDITH   But are you sure she's not giving when you
            think she's taking?

ASHLEY   No – she's taking. I'm giving.

JUDITH   Yes, I see . . . Well, Jo doesn't doubt that
            you're a giver, Ashley – her concern is
            that you may be giving it to someone else.
            (*Pause.*) Have you been doing that?

ASHLEY   (*hesitates*) How do I know she's not doing it
            to me?

JUDITH   You're not answering the question, Ashley.
            Have you? Have you been doing the very
            thing that you condemned Jo for – and in
            such violent terms.

ASHLEY   (*pause*) Yes.

JUDITH   Why?

ASHLEY   Because she's been unfaithful – or if she
              hasn't, she will be.

JUDITH   (*dryly*) So you're getting you're retaliation in
              first?

ASHLEY   You could say that.

JUDITH   That's not the real reason, is it?

ASHLEY   Isn't it?

JUDITH   This desire to be liked – to be admired by
              women – doesn't it go back a long way –
              long before Jo? Doesn't it spring from a lack
              of confidence, some insecurity and a need
              for reassurance?

              (ASHLEY *stands abruptly.*)

ASHLEY   My God! Fancy you spotting that. Fancy you
              spotting my insecurity.

JUDITH   Doesn't it go back to your childhood?

ASHLEY   (*surprised*) Yes, it does. (*Slowly.*) Hard to
              believe now but I was an ugly duckling. I
              had this vitamin deficiency. I had to wear
              callipers until my early teens. Still, that's in
              the past now.

JUDITH   Is it? Aren't you still that little boy in leg
              irons?

ASHLEY   (*alarmed*) What! No! (*He looks down.*) You
              can't see anything wrong, can you?

JUDITH   Of course not. I mean isn't that why you're
              still trying to prove yourself – still trying to
              catch up? Isn't that why you try to win every
              attractive woman you meet?

ASHLEY   No. (*Pause.*) They don't have to be attractive.

JUDITH   They don't?

ASHLEY   Just different.

JUDITH   The one who left the lipstick – was she
              different?

ASHLEY   Yes.

JUDITH   What attracted you?

ASHLEY   Something happens. I can't explain it. It's a
              sort of moment – a glance – a smile – like a
              light coming on. Then it's off to the races.
              Know what I mean?

              (JUDITH *drops her eyes and takes up her
              drink.*)

JUDITH   Yes, I know what you mean. And I think if
              you wish to keep Jo, you must stop going to
              the races. You do love her?

ASHLEY   Yes.

JUDITH   Then value her – don't lose her. Don't be
              like the base Indian who threw a pearl away
              richer than all his tribe.

ASHLEY   What?

JUDITH   You have to be honest with her. Tell her
              about the girl.

ASHLEY   She'll go mad.

JUDITH   Ashley, she's going mad not knowing. She
              wants you to be honest. She's ready to
              forgive you. Tell her about the girl – and,
              more importantly, tell her you'll never do it
              again. Can you make that promise?

ASHLEY   I think so.

JUDITH   Good. And Ashley, be patient. She may
              not be giving because she's frightened –
              frightened of being taken over – of losing
              her identity – frightened of your intensity.

ASHLEY   You're right. I am too intense. I must learn
              to relax, Judith.

JUDITH   I'll send Jo through . . .

              (*She crosses as* GERRY *appears.*)

              Where's Jo?

GERRY   Talking to her sister. I've reconnected the
              phone.

JUDITH   Oh. I don't want her to leave until she's seen
              Ashley . . .

              (*She exits.* GERRY *crosses for a drink.*)

ASHLEY   What was she saying to her sister?

GERRY   I didn't stay to listen.

ASHLEY   All right – what did she say to you – about
              me?

GERRY   You weren't mentioned.

ASHLEY   (*doubtfully*) Wasn't I? Then what did you
                 talk about? You must have talked about
                 something. What was it?

GERRY   (*pauses*) Slugs.

                 (ASHLEY *stares in amazement.*)

ASHLEY   Slugs?

GERRY   I'm having trouble with slugs.

ASHLEY   (*frowns*) I've never heard her talk about
                 slugs.

GERRY   She seemed interested.

ASHLEY   (*incredulously*) In slugs?

GERRY   I said I was thinking of putting slug pellets
                 down, but the trouble with that is they
                 attract slugs from all over. You can end up
                 with more slugs than you started with –
                 mainly dead of course. We had quite a talk.

ASHLEY   About slugs?

GERRY   Yes.

ASHLEY   You mean she was posing as some sort of
                 slug expert?

GERRY   I wouldn't say that exactly.

ASHLEY   Who's she trying to impress?

GERRY   I don't know.

ASHLEY   Her usual topics are clothes and men –
              usually men. Like the guy at the salad
              trolley. Did she talk about him?

GERRY   No – just slugs.

ASHLEY   Slugs. That's not what they talk about in the
              salon.

GERRY   Ah! So she is a hairdresser.

ASHLEY   (*stares*) Why shouldn't she be a hairdresser?

GERRY   No reason.

              (*There is a long silence.*)

ASHLEY   Slugs?

GERRY   Then we got onto moles.

              (ASHLEY *puts his glass down.*)

ASHLEY   Moles! What did she say about moles?

GERRY   That no matter how much damage they did
              she could never kill one.

ASHLEY   She said that?

GERRY   Yes.

ASHLEY   She's never seen a mole.

GERRY   She must have done. She said she couldn't
              kill them because of their little pink hands
              and velvet suits.

ASHLEY   Velvet suits? She said that?

GERRY   Yes.

ASHLEY   I can't believe this. She doesn't know anything about moles or slugs. Don't let all this talk about garden pests fool you – she was trying to impress you, that's all.

GERRY   Why should she do that?

ASHLEY   That's what I'd like to know. (*He looks around the room.*) Although I think I can guess.

GERRY   (*annoyed*) Look, just because she paints her toe-nails and goes with you – it doesn't mean she can't talk about slugs, or moles, or anything else.

ASHLEY   (*stares*) What?

GERRY   There are other things in life.

ASHLEY   Slugs!

GERRY   I mean she has an enquiring mind.

ASHLEY   How do you know? You've only heard her talk about slugs.

GERRY   I mean she has another side to her. She doesn't have to be stupid just because she goes with –

               (*He breaks off.*)

ASHLEY   (*dangerously*) Who?

GERRY   (*nervously*) I can see what she sees in you, Ashley – you've got the physique – you've

got the looks but let's face it . . . you're . . .
not . . .

(*Hesitates as* ASHLEY'S *scowl deepens.*)

ASHLEY   I'm not what?

GERRY   . . . you're not a gardener.

(JUDITH *and* JO *enter.*)

JUDITH   Now, Gerry, stop monopolising Ashley. We
           must leave these two alone for a while –
           they need to talk.

GERRY   Right.

(JUDITH *picks up the tray.*)

JUDITH   We'll make some fresh coffee . . .

(*They exit.* ASHLEY *stares after* GERRY *for a
moment then turns to* JO.)

ASHLEY   I need a strong drink.

JO   Why? Have you got something unpleasant to
           say?

ASHLEY   No – I just want a drink. What about you?

JO   No – and it's not yours to give away. It's
           just like you to offer other people's drinks
           around.

ASHLEY   They can afford it. I suppose you're
           impressed with all this?

JO   Yes – aren't you?

ASHLEY	(*looks around*) No. I think it's in poor taste.
JO	Oh, you know about that sort of thing, do you?
ASHLEY	Fake beams – fake fireplace – phoney bar. Pub architecture.
JO	Then you should feel at home. You're never out of them.
ASHLEY	He's strange.
JO	Is he?
ASHLEY	Did you talk about gardening?
JO	Yes.
ASHLEY	You wouldn't even cross a lawn.
JO	Of course I would.
ASHLEY	You wouldn't. Your heels sink in and you lose your shoes. What do you think of her?
JO	Bit of a knowledge box.
ASHLEY	I don't know what she sees in him.
JO	Well, she must see something. They've been together for twenty years. She told me.
ASHLEY	That doesn't mean anything.
JO	Doesn't it?
ASHLEY	Know what keeps them together? Guilt.

JO   Guilt?

ASHLEY   They're like two people who know where
              the body's buried.

JO   What are you talking about? What body?

ASHLEY   There'll be a body – don't you worry.

JO   You're talking in riddles. You're amazing.
              You burst into a room – criticise the décor –
              then assess everyone's character at a glance.
              You should be doing her job.

ASHLEY   Do you think they're happy?

JO   Well, you don't see them throwing the
              furniture at each other, do you?

ASHLEY   He didn't even know the colour of her eyes.

JO   I bet you did. (Jo *glances at the rosettes*.)
              Looks as if she rides.

ASHLEY   She rides – she fences – she shoots – a real
              sportswoman.

JO   Is that what attracts you?

ASHLEY   Who said I was attracted?

JO   You've always been attracted to that sort
              of woman – you've told me. You have
              these fantasies of pulling them down from
              their saddles – rolling them in the hay and
              stifling their well-bred protests with a kiss.
              (*Mimics*.) "Ashley, release me – his lordship
              may return at any moment."

ASHLEY	I don't remember saying that. (*Pause.*) Are you sure you don't want a drink?
JO	Why? Are you trying to make this painless? Are you going to dump me?
ASHLEY	Dump you! I've spent the last two hours trying to get you in my car.
JO	You've spent the last two hours trying to punch me ugly.
ASHLEY	I slapped your shoulder, that's all.
JO	You know how violence frightens me. I had enough of that with my ex.
ASHLEY	I thought he was the one who'd had enough.
JO	He'd have me back tomorrow.
ASHLEY	Then why has he changed the locks?
JO	To prevent me removing the carpet I paid for. If you remember, we're living on bare boards.
ASHLEY	I can't help being laid off.
JO	I don't care if you're laid off – laid back or laid out. I mean, where are we going? What plans have you got for the future apart from breathing?
ASHLEY	There's not much call for scaffolding at the moment. The trade's going through a bad time.

Jo   So am I! So do me a favour. The next time
             you build some scaffolding – go to the top
             and jump off.

             (*There's a silence.*)

Ashley   Have you noticed something?

Jo   What?

Ashley   I didn't react.

Jo   (*surprised*) No, you didn't, did you?

Ashley   You provoked me but I controlled myself.

Jo   I knew there was something missing – it was
             your hands round my windpipe.

Ashley   I'll never do that again.

Jo   Good.

Ashley   She made me realise. I've been trying
             to prove something – I've been seeking
             reassurance. It goes back a long way.

Jo   Did you tell her about the brave little boy –
             clanking around in callipers?

Ashley   (*smiles*) I know you're goading me but it
             won't work. I'll never hit you again.

Jo   (*stares*) Never?

Ashley   Never.

Jo   Suppose you lose your temper?

ASHLEY   I won't. That's my insecurity. Now I've
                recognised it – there won't be a problem. I
                don't know why I didn't see it before.

JO   And you'll never be violent?

ASHLEY   Never.

JO   No matter what?

ASHLEY   No.

                (*She hits him.*)

                (*smiles*) See what I mean?

                (*She hits him again. His smile becomes a
                little grim.*)

                That's the way it's going to be from now on.

                (*She hits him even harder.* ASHLEY *clenches
                his teeth.*)

                There's no need to take advantage.

JO   That was for the speech in the car park. For
                someone who's failing to communicate you
                certainly expressed yourself well there.

ASHLEY   I didn't mean it. I didn't stop to think.

JO   You didn't have to. It came out in a stream.
                You didn't even pause for breath – and
                you never used the same word twice. I've
                never known such eloquence. I think you'd
                rehearsed it in front of a mirror.

                (ASHLEY *puts his arm around her.*)

ASHLEY   That's all behind us now, Jo. I don't want to
            be like the base Indian.

JO   What?

ASHLEY   The one who threw a pearl away richer that
            all his tribe.

            (JO *stares at him in astonishment.*)

JO   Where did he come from?

ASHLEY   That's the way I feel about you.

JO   I mean where did the base Indian come
            from?

ASHLEY   I heard it somewhere.

JO   Not on the top of scaffolding, you didn't.
            She said it.

ASHLEY   Who?

JO   The knowledge box.

ASHLEY   Well, yes – but she knows what she's talking
            about. (*Gently.*) She made me realise I was
            frightened of losing you.

JO   (*softly*) Me too . . .

            (*They kiss.*)

ASHLEY   We've got to be positive.

JO   Recognise the good things.

ASHLEY   I'm recognising them now.

JO	So am I.
ASHLEY	I've been a fool. I'll never be unfaithful again.
JO	Again?
	(*She pushes him slowly back.*)
	What do you mean, again? You've only known me five minutes.
ASHLEY	Judith said we should make a fresh start – that our relationship should be open and honest . . .
JO	Go on.
ASHLEY	The lipstick. It wasn't yours.
JO	I know that.
ASHLEY	There was someone but it's all over now.
JO	Who was it?
ASHLEY	The woman from Smith's.
JO	W. H. Smith?
ASHLEY	Yes.
JO	I knew it! The one on the video counter.
ASHLEY	No. Books and Stationery.
JO	She's ninety.
ASHLEY	The other one.

JO   The fat one?

ASHLEY   Yes.

JO   (*appalled*) You've been unfaithful with a fat
              woman?

ASHLEY   She can't help it.

JO   Of course she can. She eats too much.

ASHLEY   No, it's her glands.

JO   There's not much wrong with her glands
              from what you've been saying. But I'd get
              yours checked, they seem out of control. I
              didn't know you were into fat.

ASHLEY   I'm not. I've never been with one before.

JO   So you thought it would make a change?

ASHLEY   It wasn't like that.

JO   Then what was it like?

ASHLEY   Well, I've had a lot of time on my hands
              since I've been laid off . . .

JO   Why didn't you decorate the flat?

ASHLEY   I was going to.

JO   But this cropped up!

ASHLEY   It was one lunchtime and you weren't home
              and the flat seemed empty without you . . .

Jo	So you thought you'd fill it – and I mean fill it!
ASHLEY	I was in Smith's and it started to rain . . .
Jo	What's the state of the weather got to do with it? Or does rain turn you on?
ASHLEY	I'm trying to explain. I was standing by the stationery counter when I noticed she'd been crying. I heard the others talking. The poor kid had been jilted.
Jo	Oh dear.
ASHLEY	Her fiancé had finished with her.
Jo	Probably because of her habit of jumping on the customers.
ASHLEY	It was because she'd dropped out of Weight Watchers and her fiancé was furious. She was suicidal. I walked out of the shop with her. It was raining – I didn't like to leave her.
Jo	So you took her to our place.
ASHLEY	To comfort her.
Jo	So it was a humanitarian gesture, really?
ASHLEY	In a way. I wanted to give her something to live for.
Jo	(incredulously) What?
ASHLEY	She didn't mean anything to me, Jo.

JO   You were just building up her confidence?

ASHLEY   In a way. When all the staff saw her come
                back into the shop, laughing and talking
                with this good looking fellow . . .

JO   Who was that?

ASHLEY   (*frowns*) Me.

JO   Why were you laughing?

ASHLEY   I don't know. But the girls didn't feel sorry
                for her anymore. And she felt better about
                herself. Now her boyfriend's jealous and
                wants her back . . .

JO   My God!

ASHLEY   I didn't have to tell you.

JO   The fat girl from Boots.

ASHLEY   Smith's.

JO   I don't care if it was Marks and bloody
                Spencers. I feel degraded. I bet you were
                laughing at me.

ASHLEY   No. I've always regretted it but Judith said
                we should be honest with each other.

                (JO *studies him for a moment.*)

JO   Perhaps you're right.

ASHLEY   You think so?

JO   Perhaps I should be honest with you . . .

ASHLEY	What?
JO	The man at the salad trolley . . .
ASHLEY	Yes?
JO	We didn't meet by accident.
ASHLEY	Go on.
JO	We'd met before. He came into the salon to use the sunbed. I took him a cup of tea . . .
ASHLEY	Well?
JO	Wonderful physique . . .
ASHLEY	(*shrugs*) So have I.
JO	Not an ounce of fat . . .
ASHLEY	So what?
JO	And there was something else – I couldn't help noticing . . .
ASHLEY	What?
JO	He had great legs . . .
ASHLEY	You bitch!

(*He makes a grab at her. She kicks him. They struggle. She breaks away. The furnituer goes flying. He catches her. She knees him. They collapse on the sofa. He has his hands around her throat. Curtain. End of Act One.*)

ACT TWO

Scene One

*The den, a few minutes later. The room is empty. A chair
has been knocked over – cushions are scattered on the
floor.*

*JUDITH and GERRY enter with the coffee. They are both
smiling expectantly. Their smiles fade. They stare about
them and then at each other. GERRY crosses and looks out of
the window.*

GERRY   Where are they?

JUDITH   They must have left.

GERRY   Without saying anything?

JUDITH   That can be a good sign. When they
             dispense with the counsellor – ignore her
             – even despise her. It show's she's done her
             job in bringing them together.

GERRY   Perhaps – or it may mean that they simply
             despise her.

JUDITH   What are you suggesting?

GERRY   That you're not always successful.

JUDITH   I know that.

GERRY   Remember that errant husband who threw
             a chair at you? His wife had to leap on his
             back to restrain him.

JUDITH   (*shrugs*) At least I brought them together.

             (GERRY *picks up the chair.*)

GERRY   Looks as if there may have been some chair
               throwing around here . . .

               (JUDITH *starts to tidy the room.*)

JUDITH   Are you suggesting that he's attacked Jo and
               driven off with her?

GERRY   He hasn't driven off. I don't like to think of
               the other possibilities.

JUDITH   He wouldn't harm her, Gerry.

GERRY   He's attacked her once.

JUDITH   That was a cry for help.

GERRY   What a cliché!

JUDITH   I'm sorry I'm talking in clichés.

GERRY   Don't be. After all, he is a cliché, isn't he?

JUDITH   Ashley? A few minutes ago I thought you
               were ready to adopt him. Can't you see he's
               being manipulated?

GERRY   Manipulated! She's the one who's being
               manipulated. She was married at seventeen.
               She never had a chance. Men have always
               manipulated her.

JUDITH   Did she tell you that?

GERRY   Yes.

JUDITH   I thought you talked about garden pests.

GERRY   We did. We went from garden pests to men –
          it seemed a natural development.

          (*She studies him.*)

JUDITH   Oh dear. It seems you're off men altogether.
          Did Ashley do that?

GERRY   He's scary, Judith.

JUDITH   I thought you said he was a cliché.

GERRY   He's a scary cliché. Look what he did to that
          door. He's violent. Think what he could have
          done to her. (*Pause.*) And he keeps asking
          questions about you . . .

JUDITH   About me?

GERRY   The colour of your eyes – that sort of thing.
          He thinks they're grey.

JUDITH   They are grey.

GERRY   Oh.

JUDITH   What's wrong with asking about the colour
          of my eyes?

GERRY   Nothing. (*Pause.*) But when we were alone
          in the study he asked something else . . .

JUDITH   What?

GERRY   You're not going to like this.

JUDITH   Go on.

GERRY   He asked what you were like in bed.

JUDITH	What! (*Angrily.*) Who does he think he is?
GERRY	Exactly.
JUDITH	(*pause*) What did you say?
GERRY	I said you were perfectly normal.
JUDITH	(*stares*) Normal?
GERRY	I didn't want to arouse his interest.
JUDITH	You certainly wouldn't – not with normal. I'm surprised you didn't say adequate.
GERRY	Well, it's obvious we get along – all the years we've been together.
JUDITH	(*stares again*) Get along! I think I prefer normal (*Frowns.*) Why do you keep staring out of the window?
GERRY	I hope nothing's happened to her.
JUDITH	If it has, I'm sure it will be all perfectly normal.
GERRY	What?
JUDITH	She's charmed you, hasn't she?
GERRY	No.
JUDITH	Well, it's not for want of trying. If there was no-one else in the room she'd flirt with the sideboard. I suppose she's impressed by you. Ashley's out of work – and you're a success in life.

GERRY   No. I'm a success in business – that's not the
            same thing.

JUDITH   What made you say that? You've never said
            that before.

            (GERRY *begins to pace the room.*)

GERRY   We should never have left them together.
            Worst thing we could have done. What will
            the police say?

JUDITH   Police?

GERRY   If something's happened to that poor girl.

JUDITH   Nothing's happened to her. They've
            probably driven home.

            (*She crosses to the hall.*)

GERRY   They haven't.

JUDITH   (*stops*) How do you know?

GERRY   Because I've immobilised his car.

            (*She turns back.*)

JUDITH   You've done what?

GERRY   Immobilised his car.

JUDITH   (*stares*) You don't know how to immobilize
            a car – you don't know anything about cars.

GERRY   I do.

JUDITH   What did you do?

GERRY   I jammed a potato into the exhaust pipe – it
               prevents it from firing.

               (JUDITH *stares at him in total astonishment.*)

JUDITH   A potato?

GERRY   Yes.

JUDITH   Let me get this straight. You crept out there
               and jammed a potato into his exhaust pipe?

GERRY   Yes.

JUDITH   Why?

GERRY   To immobilize the car.

JUDITH   I know that! But I find the idea of you
               creeping out there with a car-immobilizing
               potato rather strange. It's not as if you've
               been in the army. And why should you
               wish to immobilize the car? I thought you
               couldn't wait to get rid of him.

GERRY   I didn't want him to abduct her. I didn't
               want her finishing up in his boot.
               Remember, I saw that happen. That woman
               went in very easily – and she was alive . . .

JUDITH   (*alarmed*) Alive? What are you suggesting,
               Gerry?

GERRY   That we could be dealing with a
               psychopath . . .

               (*His voice dies away as* ASHLEY *enters from
               the hall.* ASHLEY *has a scratch on his cheek.
               He is wiping his hands on an oily rag.*)

ASHLEY   I can't understand it. The car won't start.
                I've checked everything. Battery, plugs,
                starter. It's never happened before.

GERRY   (*uneasily*) Perhaps I could take a look.

ASHLEY   Do you know anything about cars?

JUDITH   (*dryly*) He knows about exhausts.

GERRY   Let me check it over while you wash your
                hands. (*Casually.*) Is Jo out there?

ASHLEY   Jo?

GERRY   Isn't she with you?

ASHLEY   No. I thought she was with you. She came
                back to say goodbye.

                (JUDITH *and* GERRY *glance at each other.*)

JUDITH   Ashley, there's nothing wrong is there?

ASHLEY   No. You were right. We were failing to
                communicate – that was our problem. She
                couldn't see I needed reassurance. I couldn't
                see she needed space. Well, she's given me
                the reassurance and I've given her the space.

                (*He becomes aware of* JUDITH'S *stare.*)

                What's the matter?

JUDITH   You have a scratch on your face.

ASHLEY   I caught it on the bonnet of the car. (*Looks
                at his hands.*) Across the hall?

JUDITH   On the right. Let me take your jacket.

                (*She removes his jacket.*)

                I'll pour you some coffee . . .

                (ASHLEY *exits.* GERRY *makes sure the door is closed.*)

GERRY   Reassurance! I've never known anyone in less need of reassurance. And as for the space he's given her – that could be the width of a car boot.

JUDITH   Don't be ridiculous, Gerry.

GERRY   His face was scratched.

JUDITH   He explained that.

GERRY   Not to my satisfaction. He's hiding something.

JUDITH   Gerry, they were only alone for a few minutes.

GERRY   That's all it takes.

JUDITH   She must have walked home.

GERRY   Then why is her coat still here?

JUDITH   She must have forgotten it.

GERRY   I don't think so.

JUDITH   Then where is she?

GERRY   Where do you think?

JUDITH   (*sighs*) Not the car boot again.

GERRY   He hasn't had time to dispose of her. It
                would be the boot – quick and easy. Drive
                off as if nothing's happened. A year later
                she's identified by her dental records. We
                should ring the police.

JUDITH   And wouldn't you look silly if a moment
                later she walked through that door.

GERRY   I wouldn't mind looking silly. I'd rejoice in
                it. I'd give anything to see her walk through
                that door.

JUDITH   You're becoming hysterical.

GERRY   Am I? Are you sure it's not you who's afraid
                to look silly. Ten minutes counselling from
                you and a minor tiff becomes a full scale
                murder hunt.

JUDITH   (*sighs*) Very well, if it'll make you feel any
                better – I'll look in the boot.

GERRY   He didn't give me the keys.

JUDITH   Perhaps they're in his jacket pocket?

GERRY   (*hesitates*) Do you think I should look?

JUDITH   Gerry, if I'm prepared to look in the boot,
                surely you can look in his jacket pocket . . .

                (*She crosses and listens at the door.* GERRY
                *gingerly searches the pockets. He takes an
                object from the pocket with deep disgust.*)

GERRY   Just look at this.

JUDITH   What is it?

GERRY   A packet of three. Obviously picked them
                up from the men's room. Probably thought
                he might get lucky on the way home. He's
                a sexual opportunist. (*Feels in top pocket.*)
                And look at this pen. It has a dancing girl
                on it – when it's turned upside down she
                undresses. No doubt about it, he's obsessed.

JUDITH   You're supposed to be looking for his keys.

GERRY   Here they are.

                (*He hands the keys to* JUDITH. *Shivers.*)

JUDITH   What's the matter?

GERRY   The thought of her lying there all crumpled.

JUDITH   (*tartly*) I thought she looked fairly crumpled
                when she arrived.

GERRY   She was not. She was alive and vital.

JUDITH   Well, we'll soon know.

GERRY   I'll keep him talking.

JUDITH   I thought you might.

GERRY   When you come back – we'll need a signal.

JUDITH   A signal?

GERRY   If she's there . . . in the boot . . . (*Winces.*)
                Give me a sign – so I can make a call – then
                you keep him talking.

JUDITH	Oh, now I can keep him talking – now he's a murderer.
GERRY	He listens to you.
JUDITH	What sort of sign?
GERRY	If she's there . . . yawn.
JUDITH	Yawn?
GERRY	Yawn elaborately – as if you're bored – that won't arouse suspicion.
JUDITH	Gerry, I've got news for you – I am bored – I'm yawning right now.

(*She exits onto terrace.* GERRY *closes the door after her. He is following her progress as* ASHLEY *returns and slips on his jacket. he begins to feel in his pockets.*)

| ASHLEY | Do you want the keys? |

(GERRY *turns hastily.*)

GERRY	No.
ASHLEY	I thought you were going to look at the car?
GERRY	Plenty of time. Let's have a drink.

(*He crosses to the bar.* ASHLEY *continues feeling in his pockets.*)

| ASHLEY | That's funny. They're not here. |
| GERRY | What? |

ASHLEY   My keys.

GERRY   You probably dropped them in the drive.

ASHLEY   I distinctly remember putting them in my
             pocket.

GERRY   That's always happening to me. Distinctly
             remember putting them in my pocket and
             they turn up somewhere else. You're lost
             without your car keys. I can enter a room
             full of confidence – feel for my car keys –
             not there – total panic – a gibbering wreck
             in no time.

             (*His voice dies away as he realises that*
             ASHLEY *is watching him curiously.*)

             Same again?

             (*He pours* ASHLEY *a drink.* ASHLEY *crosses
             to the window.*)

ASHLEY   Where's Judith?

GERRY   Judith? Looking for Jo. (*Pause.*) You
             quarrelled, didn't you?

ASHLEY   Did we?

GERRY   Why didn't you say so?

ASHLEY   (*shrugs*) I didn't want to disappoint Judith.
             (*Takes drink.*) How tall is she?

GERRY   Who?

ASHLEY   Your wife.

GERRY   I don't know.

ASHLEY   (*stares*) You don't know how tall she is?

GERRY   I haven't measured her. (*Hesitates.*) I used to
             know . . . I think she may have shrunk.

ASHLEY   I'm not surprised . . . marriage can do that.
             I've noticed that about married couples –
             most of them are round shouldered.

             (GERRY *straightens.*)

ASHLEY   I don't insist on a woman being tall but I
             like long legs. I have a definite weakness for
             long legs. On the other hand short women
             can spring a few surprises – they can often
             provide the unexpected.

GERRY   I didn't know that.

ASHLEY   (*pause*) Ever been with a fat woman?

GERRY   No – I can't say I have.

ASHLEY   That's different.

GERRY   Is it?

ASHLEY   Not to be underrated. Highly prized in the
             East. Arabs stuff them with sweetmeats.

GERRY   So I understand.

ASHLEY   Not in the West. It's all dictated by fashion.
             Fashion's hard on fat women.

GERRY   I suppose it is.

ASHLEY   It doesn't mean they don't have emotions.
             The idea that they're having a love affair
             with food is totally erroneous. And they
             can be extremely graceful. Have you seen a
             fat woman dance – astonishingly lithe. And
             they're responsive. Fat women take their
             chances – know what I mean, Gerry?

GERRY   I know what you mean, Ashley.

             (JUDITH *enters. She crosses and hands*
             ASHLEY *his keys.*)

JUDITH   I found your keys in the drive.

ASHLEY   No sign of her then?

JUDITH   What?

ASHLEY   Jo. No sign of her?

JUDITH   No.

             (GERRY *has become agitated. He searches*
             JUDITH'S *face for some indication. She*
             glances at him for a moment and then yawns
             elaborately. GERRY *groans and slumps into*
             a chair as if all the strength has gone out of
             his legs. ASHLEY *turns and looks at him in*
             surprise.)

ASHLEY   What's the matter with Gerry?

             (GERRY *looks blankly ahead.*)

JUDITH   (*quickly*) Too much to drink, I'm afraid. It's
             been a hectic night.

ASHLEY   Well, he's certainly in no condition to look
             at the car. I'll try again . . .

(*He exits through hall.*)

GERRY   (*emotionally*) For God's sake, ring the
             police, don't let him get away with it. (*He
             dabs his eyes with a handkerchief.*)

JUDITH   Gerry – are you crying?

GERRY   Of course I'm crying. That beautiful girl.
             And it's all your fault. Why did you have to
             meddle? No wonder that man threw a chair
             at you.

JUDITH   He was mentally disturbed.

GERRY   It was the sanest thing he ever did. I'm
             surprised you're not dodging chairs on a
             daily basis. What gives you the right to
             advise people? It's not as if you're any good
             at it yourself. When I think of that poor girl
             – gone forever . . .

JUDITH   (*quietly*) She wasn't there.

GERRY   (*stares*) What?

JUDITH   Jo wasn't there.

GERRY   But you yawned.

             (JUDITH *crosses to the bar.*)

JUDITH   I'm tired. I yawned because I was tired.

             (*He follows her.*)

GERRY   You yawned elaborately. That was the
             signal.

JUDITH   (*hesitates*) Was it? I was confused. I thought
              I had to yawn if she wasn't there.

              (*He regards her searchingly.*)

GERRY   You weren't confused. You're never
              confused. You did that deliberately. Why?

JUDITH   (*shrugs*) I was joking.

GERRY   Joking! Over a thing like that?

JUDITH   I know it was in bad taste. But I couldn't
              resist it.

GERRY   It was a cruel thing to do.

JUDITH   I know. I regretted it instantly. And I'm
              sorry.

GERRY   Sadistic.

JUDITH   (*contritely*) Yes.

              (*He stares at her, still unconvinced.*)

GERRY   That's not the truth either. You've never
              gone in for jokes – doubtful or otherwise.
              You have no sense of humour.

JUDITH   My goodness – I'm certainly finding out
              about myself tonight.

GERRY   Why did you pretend she was dead?

JUDITH   (*pause*) I suppose it was curiosity.

GERRY   Why were you curious?

JUDITH   I've never seen you like this before. You're
              normally so laid back. I wanted to see how
              much it meant to you – and it meant a great
              deal apparently.

              (GERRY *puts away the handkerchief.*)

GERRY   Judith, we were talking about someone's
              life . . .

              (ASHLEY *enters.*)

ASHLEY   I'll have to ring a garage.

JUDITH   It's late. Let Gerry look at it.

ASHLEY   Are you sure he's up to it?

JUDITH   He's feeling better now, aren't you darling?

GERRY   Yes.

              (*He takes the keys from* ASHLEY.)

              I'll see to it.

              (*He exits into hall.*)

ASHLEY   Is he all right?

JUDITH   He is now. He became rather emotional – not
              at all like him.

ASHLEY   She can do that to a man.

JUDITH   Who can?

ASHLEY   Jo. I've seen her husband's eyes red from
weeping because of her. I've seen him
reduced to wearing dark glasses in public.

JUDITH   Good heavens!

ASHLEY   That's what she can do. He had to have
psychiatric treatment – he's still under
sedation. Poor Gerry wouldn't stand a
chance. (*A pause. He regards her.*) He didn't
even know the colour of your eyes.

JUDITH   I know.

ASHLEY   Or your star sign.

JUDITH   Is that important?

ASHLEY   Oh yes. What is it?

JUDITH   Why do you want to know?

ASHLEY   I'm curious.

(*She moves away and looks out into the
garden. He follows.*)

JUDITH   She could be out there in the garden I
suppose. It's a warm evening, she could be
curled up somewhere.

ASHLEY   She could . . .

JUDITH   I think we should look for her.

ASHLEY   So do I . . .

(*She opens the door to the terrace. She
pauses.*)

JUDITH   Pisces.

ASHLEY   Incredible.

JUDITH   Why?

ASHLEY   We're in conjunction.

                (*They exit into the garden.* GERRY *enters from the hall a moment later.*)

GERRY   Fixed it.

                (*He looks around and realises they've gone. Looks out into the garden, then places the car keys onto the bar. He pours himself a drink and sits down on the padded window seat. He juggles with the potato. Slowly a look of concern crosses his face, it is followed by one of horror. He looks down at the seat and stands gingerly. He bends and slowly lifts the lid slightly hardly daring to look. He throws the lid back and begins to search. He takes out blankets, hockey stick, items of sports equipment, fencing foils, mask, bridle, etc. Lays them on the ground.* Jo *enters from the hall. She regards him curiously. She crosses and taps him on the shoulder. He shrieks and turns.*)

GERRY   Oh, God!

JO   What are you doing?

GERRY   I was looking for you.

JO   In there?

GERRY   You'd fit – I can assure you. I've seen women crammed into smaller places.

JO	If I wanted to lie down I wouldn't get into there.
GERRY	I know you wouldn't. I thought Ashley may have put you in there. I've been out of my mind with worry. What happened?
JO	(*shrugs*) His rage control button fell off again. Judith asked us to be honest with each other. That was fatal.
GERRY	Fatal?
JO	Like lighting a blue touch paper.
GERRY	Why?
JO	Everyone has something to hide.
GERRY	(*considers*) I haven't . . .
JO	(*stares*) You don't have anything to hide?
GERRY	No.
JO	Never?
GERRY	No.
	(JO *studies him.*)
JO	How does it feel?
GERRY	(*frowns*) I don't feel anything.
JO	That's what I thought.
	(GERRY *regards her.*)

GERRY   Have you always had something to hide?

JO   Ever since I can remember.

GERRY   (*pause*) How does it feel?

JO   Exciting.

(*They are quite close.* GERRY *moves away.*)

GERRY   Did he attack you?

JO   Out of the blue. Totally unexpected.

GERRY   What did he do?

JO   Tried to throttle me.

GERRY   My God!

JO   Then I kneed him in the family jewels and got out fast.

GERRY   (*shakes head*) I didn't realise people did things like that to each other.

JO   I suppose you think it's uncivilised?

GERRY   I didn't say that.

(*He begins to return the contents of the window seat.*)

Where have you been?

JO   I was walking to my sister's.

GERRY   Why did you come back?

Jo	(*shrugs*) I forgot my coat.
	(*She moves closer.* GERRY *fumbles for a cigarette, then remembers, puts it back in the packet.*)
Jo	(*curiously*) Aren't you going to smoke it?
GERRY	I only smoke in the garden. One of our ground rules.
Jo	Ground rules?
GERRY	You should have ground rules, Jo. Avoids conflict, misunderstandings and unpleasant scenes – like the one we witnessed tonight.
Jo	What sort of ground rules?
GERRY	We respect each other's no-go areas. She doesn't complain about my smoking and drinking – I don't complain about her being out all hours doing good works.
Jo	Does she do a lot of good works?
GERRY	Oh yes. Always out serving the needs of the dysfunctional. Always away on courses, learning to empathise.
Jo	Empathise?
GERRY	Feeling other's emotions – so that she can help.
Jo	So they're your ground rules? You smoke in the garden and she empathises.
GERRY	There's more to it than that. I don't make fun of her – or what she does. She is

inclined to be serious. I don't make fun of
her mother, either. In fact, I don't mention
her mother at all, well, only in reverent
tones. She has no sense of humour where
her mother's concerned – neither has her
mother. Then there are the small things
– toothpaste in the hand basin – lavatory
seat up – drumming my fingers when she's
talking – she really hates that. Have you
noticed me doing that? I can't stop myself.
And saying, "yes, yes, yes," when she's
only half way through what she's saying . . .
(*Pause.*) Why are you smiling?

JO   Most of these ground rules seem to apply to
                    you.

GERRY   (*pauses*) He was right about your eyes.

JO   What did he say?

GERRY   That they get deeper and deeper until you
                    think you're drowning but you don't care –
                    and you don't want to be saved.

JO   He said that?

GERRY   Yes.

JO   He didn't mean it. He's such a phoney.

                    (*Nevertheless* Jo *looks pleased.*)

GERRY   You're a gypsy, aren't you?

JO   My mother was but she married an
                    electrician – so don't expect me to run
                    barefoot through the woods.

GERRY   Ashley says that once you've kissed a gypsy
          woman, you never get over it.

          (Jo *glances towards the terrace.*)

JO   Well, he seems to have got over it pretty
          quick. He's such a phoney.

GERRY   Why did you go with him?

JO   I didn't know he was a phoney when I met
          him. He came into the salon to have his
          hair cut. That was a major operation. Wash,
          blow-dry, teasing . . . I should have been
          warned. But I was lonely. My old man had
          lost interest.

GERRY   (*surprised*) In you?

JO   Yes. So much for the kiss of the gypsy
          woman. Although he did want me back but
          by then it was too late. I was aching for a
          man to put his arms around me. And Ashley
          didn't need any encouragement – his were
          like tentacles.

GERRY   You? I can't believe it.

JO   You'd be surprised how many women are
          aching for some man to put his arms round
          them.

GERRY   (*pause*) Yes but which ones? I'm never sure.

JO   The odds are in your favour, Gerry.

GERRY   (*frowns*) We were talking about Ashley.

JO   Ashley doesn't seem to have any problems.

GERRY   How does he do it?

JO   He swears by body language.

GERRY   Body language?

JO   The way a woman stands – the way she
                moves . . .

                (*She moves around seductively finishing
                close to* GERRY.)

                Her closeness – the way she uses her eyes . . .

GERRY   (*clears throat*) Yes, I see.

JO   Ashley's very quick to establish a
                relationship. We'll be in a restaurant and
                he's chatting to the waitress about the meal
                – then suddenly it's where she went for her
                holidays – her star sign – and her favourite
                perfume. I'll go to get my coat – and you
                know how long that takes – when I get
                back they're talking about the size of her
                flat – problems with her boyfriend – and
                premature ejaculation.

GERRY   Good heavens!

                (JO *glances again towards the window.*)

JO   That's what's happening right now . . .

GERRY   Do you think so?

JO   Ashley's a great believer in star signs.
                What's Judith's star sign?

GERRY   I'm not sure.

JO   (*stares*) You don't know her star sign?

GERRY   I used to. I've forgotten.

JO   Well, he'll find out – and it'll be compatible
              with his.

GERRY   How do you know?

JO   Because it always is. He's such a phoney.
              They are out there, aren't they?

GERRY   They're looking for you.

JO   Do you believe that?

GERRY   Why shouldn't I?

JO   Because you haven't gone to tell them I'm
              here. You haven't looked for them. Is that
              because of the ground rules?

GERRY   No – I trust Judith.

JO   With Ashley?

GERRY   I trust her good taste.

JO   You mean Ashley's not good taste? Perhaps
              I'm not good taste.

GERRY   I didn't say that.

JO   If I go with Ashley how can I have good
              taste?

GERRY   Because you're throwing yourself away.

Jo   I've noticed that about a man – where ever
             another man's concerned he always says the
             woman's throwing herself away. (*Pause.*)
             Does Judith think I'm throwing myself
             away?

Gerry   I've no idea.

Jo   She gives a lot of advice, doesn't she?

Gerry   Well, yes – it's what she does.

Jo   Do you think you can do that?

Gerry   What?

Jo   Theorise about love?

Gerry   Judith can. She's got books on it.

Jo   It doesn't come out of a book, Gerry . . .

Gerry   (*pause*) Are you one of those women?

Jo   Which ones?

Gerry   The ones who are aching to feel a man's
             arms around them.

Jo   (*smiles*) As I've said, the odds are in your
             favour, Gerry . . .

             (*They move closer. They kiss. She regards
             him. Smiles.*)

             (*Softly.*) Now you have something to hide . . .

             (*Lights fade. Curtain.*)

Scene Two

The den. An hour later. It is now early morning. JUDITH
enters guiltily from the terrace. She is straightening her
hair and brushing her skirt. She is unaware of pieces
of grass clinging to the back of her jacket. She calls
tentatively.

JUDITH   Gerry . . . Gerry . . .

                    (*She exits into hall. A few moments later*
                    GERRY *enters from the hall equally furtively.*
                    He is hopping and pulling on a shoe. Having
                    accomplished this he crosses to the bar,
                    pours a drink and tries to take up a relaxed
                    position. He fails miserably as he becomes
                    aware that his two shoes are of a different
                    colour. JUDITH *returns. They smile uneasily*
                    at each other.)

JUDITH   There you are. We couldn't find Jo
                    anywhere. We practically searched the
                    neighbourhood. Our only conclusion is that
                    she must have walked to her sister's.

GERRY   No – she's upstairs.

JUDITH   (*stares*) Upstairs? What's she doing up
                    there?

GERRY   Repairing her make-up – etcetera.

JUDITH   Etcetera?

GERRY   She came back after you'd gone.

JUDITH   You might have told me.

GERRY   I didn't like to leave her.

JUDITH   You've left her now.

GERRY   I've hidden the sleeping tablets.

JUDITH   As distressed as that?

GERRY   Beside herself. She needed to talk to
               someone.

JUDITH   Gerry, if she needed more counselling, you
               should have come for me. It's my field.

GERRY   I would have done but she was in such a
               state – poor girl. (*Pause.*) Where's Ashley?

JUDITH   Checking his car. I told him about the
               potato.

GERRY   (*anxiously*) Was he annoyed?

JUDITH   No. He was amused.

GERRY   That doesn't sound like Ashley.

JUDITH   He's made great strides. He's recovered his
               sense of humour.

GERRY   I didn't know he had one.

JUDITH   Oh yes. Jo rather stifled it but it was always
               there. Since we've talked his improvement's
               been quite dramatic – particularly in rage
               control.

GERRY   (*relieved*) Good. I'm glad to hear it.

JUDITH   Of course, it all came from this obsessive
              jealousy.

GERRY   Has he got that under control as well?

JUDITH   Yes.

GERRY   (*more relieved*) Thank God. Then it's trebles
              all round. (*Pours drinks.*)

JUDITH   It was fuelled by his low self-esteem – he
              realises that now. Jo didn't help there. I've
              been able to enhance his self-regard.

GERRY   You have?

JUDITH   Yes. It goes back a long way. I was able to
              trace it to his childhood. He had a difficult
              time – he had to wear leg irons.

GERRY   (*alarmed*) Leg irons! You mean he was
              under restraint?

JUDITH   No. He had weak legs. He was an invalid.
              He's been over compensating for it ever
              since . . .

              (*Her voice dies away as she regards* GERRY'S
              shoes.)

              You're wearing odd shoes.

              (GERRY *looks down in surprise.*)

GERRY   Are you sure?

JUDITH   Of course I'm sure.

GERRY   No. Must be the light.

JUDITH   Gerry, one's brown and one's black. It's not
                the light.

                (GERRY *studies them.*)

GERRY   They look the same to me.

JUDITH   The same! One has a tassel.

GERRY   So it does. I wonder how that happened.

JUDITH   Did you go out like that?

GERRY   Must have done.

JUDITH   And no one noticed?

GERRY   Apparently not. Unless they were too polite
                to mention it. Of course I did have my feet
                under the table most of the time. So, you've
                really done a good job with Ashley?

JUDITH   I believe so.

GERRY   And has he got over this infidelity thing?

JUDITH   What?

GERRY   The infidelity? The serial adultery?

JUDITH   (*hesitates*) He's fighting it. But we have to
                take one step at a time.

                (*She turns away. He picks a piece of grass
                from her jacket. She turns.*)

                What was that?

GERRY   Piece of grass – on your jacket.

JUDITH	We searched everywhere . . . (*She pulls a comic face.*) Gerry, I hope you weren't worried about me – out all this time with a serial adulterer.
GERRY	(*relaxed*) Not at all.
JUDITH	Oh.
GERRY	And he's not such a bad type – underneath. And who are we to judge him. So he goes in for a little infidelity. It's not such a big deal these days.
JUDITH	(*stares*) Not such a big deal?
GERRY	These days.
JUDITH	Isn't it?
GERRY	Changing attitudes . . . people are more laid back . . .
JUDITH	More laid back?
GERRY	Well, I think a healthy relationship should be able to stand that sort of thing.
JUDITH	What sort of thing?
GERRY	The occasional infidelity.
JUDITH	Gerry, a relationship that can stand that sort of thing, isn't healthy.
GERRY	Oh, isn't it?
JUDITH	I've spent years teaching couples how to enjoy a good relationship without infidelity.

Are you saying I've been wasting my time?
(*Her voice rises.*) Really!

(*He looks at her in surprise.*)

GERRY   Sorry. Didn't mean to touch on a sore point.

JUDITH   (*angrily*) It's not a sore point!

GERRY   Didn't mean you were wasting your time. I
            meant a healthy relationship can forgive –
            start again.

JUDITH   Well, yes . . .

GERRY   I mean to err is human – to forgive is divine.

JUDITH   Yes . . . That does depend on the erring I
            imagine.

GERRY   Right. Take us.

JUDITH   (*surprised*) What?

GERRY   You and me. Easy going. Rubbing along
            very nicely.

JUDITH   Rubbing along?

GERRY   Plenty of give and take. Don't live in each
            other's pockets. Respect each other's space.
            Do our own thing. Now, if it were to happen
            to us – and I'm not saying it would – in fact,
            it's most unlikely. But if it did – it wouldn't
            be the end of the world.

JUDITH   It wouldn't?

GERRY   No. Because we have our ground rules.
             We respect each other as individuals. We
             don't try and own each other. That was Jo's
             mistake – too possessive. That's why I have
             sympathy for poor old Ashley.

JUDITH   So we're back with poor old Ashley again?

GERRY   She tried to own him.

JUDITH   Gerry, I've never heard you express this
             particular theory before. How long have you
             felt like this?

GERRY   Felt like what?

JUDITH   Doing your own thing? Whatever that might
             mean.

GERRY   Ages. And I'm going to do something about it.

JUDITH   What?

GERRY   After all, you're always away on these
             courses. I'm stuck here on my own.

JUDITH   What is it that you're going to do, Gerry?

GERRY   Fishing.

JUDITH   (*astonished*) Fishing?

GERRY   I'm going back to fishing.

JUDITH   Back? You've never been there. You've
             never fished.

GERRY   I did when I was a boy. You've always said
             I don't get out in the fresh air enough. How

pale I've been looking lately. That's the
answer. Fishing. That's what I've missed.
Being alone by the river. With just the sound
of the moorhen and the grebe . . .

JUDITH   (*stares*) The grebe? I didn't know you were
              acquainted with the grebe.

GERRY   I used to be. (*Sighs.*) I've lost touch.
              'Getting and spending we lay waste our
              powers', Judith.

JUDITH   I thought we'd been getting and spending
              quite nicely at the moment, Gerry.

GERRY   It's not enough.

JUDITH   It isn't.

GERRY   I need to get away. I need to get closer to
              nature. I need solitude. Away from business
              – from the office. I'll tell them to hold my
              calls.

JUDITH   And what about me?

GERRY   You?

JUDITH   Will I be there – with the moorhen and the
              grebe?

GERRY   No, you'd be bored. You're an active woman.
              You wouldn't want to sit there all day
              watching my float bob up and down.

JUDITH   I see. And whilst you're listening to the
              moorhen and the grebe and watching your
              float bob up and down what will I be doing?

GERRY   Need you ask? Your good works – away on
             courses . . . learning to empathise . . .

             (ASHLEY *enters from the hall.*)

JUDITH   You wouldn't believe it, Ashley. Jo's been
             here the whole time.

ASHLEY   No! And we've looked everywhere.

             (JUDITH *picks up the tray of dirty coffee
             cups.*)

JUDITH   Don't hold your breath, Ashley but we're
             finally going to have that coffee . . .

             (*She exits.* ASHLEY *regards* GERRY *who looks
             uncomfortable.*)

ASHLEY   So she was here the whole time?

GERRY   Yes.

ASHLEY   You've been crafty, haven't you?

GERRY   What?

ASHLEY   You've been . . . very crafty.

GERRY   Have I?

             (*He nervously takes out cigarette.
             Remembers and slips it back.* ASHLEY *is
             watching him.*)

ASHLEY   Butter wouldn't melt in your mouth – and all
             the time . . .

GERRY   Ashley, I –

ASHLEY   The potato.

GERRY   Potato?

ASHLEY   In the exhaust.

GERRY   Oh yes. Sorry about that.

ASHLEY   (*grins*) That's all right. I don't mind. Normally I'd have been foaming – but now look. I thought my rages were ungovernable. Now I realise they can be controlled. Judith's taught me that. She's given me back my self-respect.

GERRY   (*fervently*) Good.

ASHLEY   Only a woman can do that. She taught me that rage achieves nothing except a spiral of violence. It's negative. I've got to stop listening to those voices.

GERRY   (*uneasily*) What voices, Ashley?

ASHLEY   The voices that say she doesn't love me. That there's someone else – another man – and the two of them are laughing at me behind my back.

GERRY   Ah, those voices . . .

ASHLEY   I've told those voices to get out of my life, Gerry.

GERRY   Great. Would you like a drink?

             (Jo *enters.* ASHLEY *moves forward.*)

JO   Don't come near me!

ASHLEY   It's all right, Jo. I'm over it.

JO   You've said that before.

ASHLEY   No – really. See how relaxed I am.

JO   You were relaxed after you'd been with that
              girl from Smith's. I'd never seen anyone so
              relaxed.

ASHLEY   That's a negative thought, Jo.

JO   She wasn't a negative thought when you
              were bouncing up and down on top of her –
              and I mean bouncing. And don't try and get
              round me. You're always nice to me when
              you've something to hide.

GERRY   (*desperately*) Should I mix some martinis?

              (*He edges away to the cocktail shaker and
              starts preparations.*)

ASHLEY   That's another negative thought. I can see
              it now because I've been counselled. It's
              taught me to be positive. Act affectionate
              and you'll be affectionate. Act loving – and
              you are loving. Loving becomes a reality.

JO   You mean you're faking it?

ASHLEY   No. I'm working at it. I'm thinking of the
              good things about you – the things that
              attracted me – what we call pleasers. What
              I'm doing is mirroring your good qualities
              so that you can see them. So that you'll
              respond and reflect my good qualities.

JO   (*frowns*) I would if I knew what they were.

ASHLEY   Negative, Jo – negative. We should value
                each other. I'm doing that right now. I see
                a colour in your cheek – a light in your eye
                that I haven't seen for a long time . . .

                (GERRY *becomes very active with the*
                cocktail shaker.)

                Eyes that have flashed over a thousand camp
                fires . . .

JO   I'm not a gypsy.

ASHLEY   You are to me. Look at her Gerry, isn't she
                magic?

                (GERRY *grins and continues shaking.*)

JO   You don't have to flatter me. There's
                nothing wrong with my self-esteem. Gerry's
                seen to that.

                (*The shaking grows intense.* ASHLEY *glances*
                curiously at GERRY.)

ASHLEY   Oh, how's that?

JO   He listened to me. He was kind and
                considerate.

                (JUDITH *calls from the kitchen.* GERRY *puts*
                down the shaker.)

GERRY   I'll see how the coffee's coming along . . .

                (*He crosses between them.* JO *takes his*
                hand.)

JO   I want to thank you, Gerry – you've been
                wonderful.

ASHLEY   (*calmly*) And I want to thank you, too, Gerry
              – for being kind and considerate to Jo.

GERRY   That's all right.

              (GERRY *exits*.)

ASHLEY   (*pause*) Kind and considerate?

JO   Very.

ASHLEY   Good old Gerry.

JO   Kind and considerate – and attentive.

ASHLEY   He would be. He's the attentive sort. I like
              him. Pity about his shape.

JO   Shape?

ASHLEY   Funny shape.

JO   I hadn't noticed.

ASHLEY   Round-shouldered and pot-bellied. Know
              the trouble. Too many expense account
              lunches. That would never happen to me.

JO   You're right there. Who's going to buy you a
              business lunch?

ASHLEY   That's true. Still, when you meet someone
              like that you must thank God you've got me.

JO   Why?

ASHLEY   Well, there's no comparison, is there? (*He
              checks his reflection in the window.*) I

bet that's what you think. Thank God for
Ashley.

JO   Well, I don't. And stop trying to see
              yourself in the glass.

              (ASHLEY *turns from the window.*)

ASHLEY   Mind you, he's a good listener – no doubt
              about that. Some people are – some people
              aren't. I've always been a talker.

JO   I've noticed that.

ASHLEY   But it is a social attribute, being a good
              listener. And he's a good listener. Must be.
              How long was he listening?

JO   How long were you out there?

ASHLEY   About an hour.

JO   That's how long he was listening. What were
              you doing?

ASHLEY   Looking for you.

JO   I thought you were being counselled?

ASHLEY   That as well. She's doing wonders for me.
              She's going to get me some soothing tapes.

JO   Soothing tapes?

ASHLEY   Yes, so that when I get tense and angry I
              can listen to them in a darkened room. She's
              very understanding.

JO   Did you tell her about the time you had
              rickets?

ASHLEY   (*frowns*) I didn't have rickets.

JO   How your mother neglected you – and boiled
              all the goodness out of your greens – how
              she never really loved you or kissed you
              goodnight. How she left you to cross busy
              roads in your callipers?

ASHLEY   (*calmly*) Jo, you should avoid these remarks
              – apart from them being wounding – it's an
              area of conflict. (*Solemnly.*) You're throwing
              me into a shame spiral.

JO   (*amused*) A shame spiral!

ASHLEY   I have to feel validated, Jo.

JO   Validated! You don't even know what it
              means.

ASHLEY   It means you're the co-author of my
              insecurity.

JO   You're quoting her again, aren't you? You'd
              never have thought that up yourself.

ASHLEY   You should concentrate on the things
              about me that please you. You missed an
              opportunity just now. I know you admire my
              physique. You should have expressed that
              thought. That would have pleased me.

JO   I bet it would.

ASHLEY   You missed your opportunity.

JO   And did you miss your opportunity out
                     there?

ASHLEY   What do you mean?

JO   You know what I mean – at the risk of being
                     negative . . .

ASHLEY   Precisely! Look, you were upstairs when we
                     got back – possibly in the bedroom – am I
                     asking questions? No. Why shouldn't you be
                     upstairs in the bedroom? There would have
                     been a time when I'd have erupted. Look at
                     me now.

JO   You're a quick learner, I'll say that for you.

ASHLEY   And he was probably in the bedroom with
                     you.

JO   You mean the round-shouldered, pot-bellied
                     listener?

ASHLEY   Yes.

JO   Yes. He was as a matter of fact.

ASHLEY   And why not? Being kind, considerate and
                     attentive. I should thank him.

JO   And was Judith being kind, considerate and
                     attentive?

ASHLEY   Yes. (*Confidentially.*) And I'll tell you
                     something that might surprise you – she's
                     not happy.

JO   That does surprise me. I thought she was an
                     expert.

ASHLEY   Apparently, he doesn't understand her
              needs – he lacks emotion. He's incapable of
              deep feeling. That makes her feel cold and
              unattractive.

JO   That surprises me even more.

ASHLEY   Why?

JO   He made me feel attractive – and I found
              him warm and emotional . . .

              (ASHLEY *regards her for a moment and then
              breaks into a smile.*)

ASHLEY   Ah, I see what's happening here. You're
              testing me, aren't you? You can't believe
              I've changed. You're trying to make me
              jealous. That's good, very good. It shows the
              therapy's working. Where's the rage? There
              isn't any. That's counselling for you.

              (GERRY *enters with a plate of sandwiches.*)

GERRY   Judith's decided to do some sandwiches as
              well. Something's given her an appetite.

              (JO *raises her eyebrows.* ASHLEY *takes the
              sandwiches from* GERRY *and puts them on
              the coffee table.*)

ASHLEY   Thanks, Gerry . . .

              (*He catches sight of* GERRY'S *shoes and
              stares.* GERRY *looks uncomfortable.*)

GERRY   I'll fetch the coffee . . .

              (*He exits awkwardly.*)

ASHLEY   (*frowns*) He was wearing odd shoes.

JO   Was he?

ASHLEY   I hadn't noticed that before, had you?

JO   No.

ASHLEY   (*casually*) What was it like upstairs?

JO   Well, I only saw the master bedroom –
              bathroom en suite, of course.

ASHLEY   Of course.

JO   King sized bed – with heart shaped cushions
              – silk drapes – and over the bed – a nude.

ASHLEY   A nude?

JO   Yes, Gerry likes nudes. Surprising isn't it?

              (GERRY *enters with tray of coffee. There's
              no room on the coffee table. He stands
              uncertainly between* JO *and* ASHLEY.)

ASHLEY   (*pause*) King sized bed . . . ?

JO   Amazingly comfortable . . .

ASHLEY   Comfortable?

              (*She studies him.*)

JO   You know, you really have improved.
              Normally you'd have been grinding your
              teeth, opening and closing those big fists,
              and scowling . . .

(ASHLEY *has begun to show all these symptoms. The cups on* GERRY'S *tray begin to rattle.*)

This counselling really does work.

ASHLEY   (*through clenched teeth*) And were you the only one who found the bed comfortable?

JO   You're not suggesting . . . ?

ASHLEY   (*grimly*) He took his shoes off, didn't he?

JO   Did he?

                (*The rattle of the tea cups grows louder.*)

ASHLEY   What else did he take off?

                (JUDITH *enters smiling as* JO *begins to back away.*)

JO   Are you sure you're ready for this, Ashley? I know you've come along way but are you sure you don't want to listen to some soothing tapes? Or perhaps you need a little counselling.

                (ASHLEY *is controlling himself with a great effort.*)

                But it wasn't counselling, was it? And you weren't looking for me because she was on her back. I can tell by her smile what happened.

                (GERRY *gives* JUDITH *a surprised look.* JUDITH'S *smile disappears abruptly.* ASHLEY *begins to breath heavily.*)

ASHLEY   I think we'd better leave.

JO   Why are you breathing like that?

JUDITH   I advised Ashley to breath deeply if
                he found himself in the grip of strong
                emotions.

ASHLEY   That's all right, Judith. I've got it under
                control . . .

                (ASHLEY *is breathing furiously accompanied
                by* GERRY'S *tinkling coffee cups.*)

JO   Have you?

                (*She crosses to* GERRY *and gives him a long
                kiss on the lips. The cups almost fly off the
                tray.*)

                You were wonderful, Gerry – and I mean
                that.

                (*As she moves away* ASHLEY *lets out a roar
                of rage. He lunges for* JO. *The tray goes
                flying. In a moment* JO *and* ASHLEY *are
                wrestling around the room. He is shaking
                her. She is kicking him.*

                JUDITH *is busy trying to protect the furniture
                which is being knocked in all directions.
                Finally* JO *and* ASHLEY *crash down on the
                sofa.* GERRY *snatches up one of the fencing
                foils.*)

GERRY   (*shouts*) Stop! Take your hands of her.

                (ASHLEY *straightens up slowly, eyeing the
                foil.*)

ASHLEY   What if I don't?

GERRY   Then I'll run you through with this.

JUDITH   (*dryly*) You can't run him through with that,
           Gerry – it has a button on the end.

           (GERRY *slashes the air with the foil.*)

GERRY   Then I'll poke his eyes out.

JUDITH   Gerry – for heaven's sake.

GERRY   I'm tired of him throwing his weight around
           in my house. I didn't ask him here – and he's
           leaving. And if he doesn't . . . I'm going to
           kebab him.

           (*He makes a lunge.* ASHLEY *moves behind* Jo.)

Jo   Keep calm, Gerry. He wasn't going to hurt
           me – not really.

GERRY   He'd better not.

JUDITH   Gerry, what's happening to you?

GERRY   Gerry! Don't you mean darling?

JUDITH   I've never seen you like this.

ASHLEY   That's what she can do to men. She brings
           out the animal. He's trying to impress her.
           Well, that's easy with a sword in his hand
           against an unarmed man.

           (GERRY *hesitates then snatches up the other
           foil and hands it to* ASHLEY.)

GERRY   Now we're even.

ASHLEY   (*hesitates*) Hang about. Duelling's illegal.

GERRY   So is breaking into my house.

ASHLEY   You could go to prison.

GERRY   Do you think I care?

                    (ASHLEY *throws down the foil.*)

ASHLEY   Let's get out of here, Jo. I know you hate
                    violence . . .

                    (*He backs out of the door onto the terrace.*
                    Jo *turns to follow.*)

GERRY   Jo!

                    (*She turns back and crosses to them.*)

JO   I think the counselling's working, Judith.
                    Ashley's certainly much calmer, isn't he?
                    Although I'm not so sure about Gerry.

                    (*She kisses* GERRY *lightly on the lips.*)

                    You know, Gerry – it looks as if you'll have
                    to extend those ground rules . . .

                    (*She exits after* ASHLEY. JUDITH *and* GERRY
                    *regard each other in silence for a moment
                    and then begin to tidy the room.*)

JUDITH   (*shortly*) What a scene.

GERRY   (*uneasily*) Yes.

JUDITH

What did she mean about our ground rules?

GERRY

I was telling her about our ground rules.

JUDITH

Does she expect to be included in them?

GERRY

She doesn't believe in them. She doesn't believe in counselling either.

JUDITH

Really?

GERRY

She says couples know their problems – they know the solution. But when the solution's too painful they live with the problem. And that's when you get . . .

JUDITH

What?

GERRY

Ground rules.

JUDITH

Do we have a problem?

GERRY

Of course not . . .

JUDITH

(*sniffs*) A girl like that.

GERRY

And what about a man like that?

JUDITH

A tart.

GERRY

A scaffolder.

JUDITH

Oh. Does that worry you?

GERRY

It obviously didn't worry you.

JUDITH

What do you mean?

GERRY   Do you know what I'm thinking? All those
             courses you go on. What happens when all
             you empathisers get together?

JUDITH   I don't know what you're talking about.

GERRY   Don't you. And then I think of all those
             excuses.

JUDITH   What excuses?

GERRY   It's either too hot or too cold. Too early or
             too late. Or mother's in the next room. Or
             I've taken two sleeping tablets. Or it's not
             the weekend . . .

JUDITH   Have you been keeping a list?

GERRY   Yes. And there's one more – now what is it?

JUDITH   Don't you ever think of anything else?

GERRY   That's the one!

JUDITH   We have a perfectly normal love life.

GERRY   I don't want normal – I want lobster
             thermidor!

JUDITH   Lobster thermidor? What are you talking
             about?

GERRY   You've no idea, have you?

             (*He takes out a cigarette and puts it
             defiantly to his lips.* JUDITH *crosses and
             snatches the cigarette from his lips. She
             throws it to the floor and tramples on it.*)

JUDITH   (*scornfully*) Lobster thermidor. It would be
                wasted on you. Do you know what Ashley
                says? You drink too much and you smoke
                too much. And he's seen more life on a
                fishmonger's slab. And I can see what he
                means.

GERRY   Why . . . you . ...

                (*He seizes her and shakes her. They wrestle,
                knocking over the furniture. They fall on
                the sofa fighting and kicking.* GERRY *finally
                seizes her by the throat. The scene becomes
                a replica of the first act.* JO *and* ASHLEY
                tiptoe in from the terrace to retrieve JO'S
                coat. GERRY *still has his hands around*
                JUDITH'S *throat.*)

JO   (*apologetically*) My coat . . .

                (JUDITH *gives a sob. She breaks free and
                dashes from the room.*)

GERRY   Judith!

                (*He follows her.*)

                (JO *and* ASHLEY *watch their departure in
                silence.*)

ASHLEY   (*finally*) Know something, Jo. Never get
                involved in other people's lives.

                (*Lights fade. Curtain. The End.*)